Test Preparation Guide for Course 2

1992 Edition

To accompany the textbook,
OPERATIONS OF LIFE AND HEALTH INSURANCE COMPANIES, Second Edition
by Kenneth Huggins, FLMI/M, and Robert D. Land, FLMI, ACS

Martha Humbard, FLMI, ACS
Project Editor

Susan Conant, FLMI, CEBS, HIA
Contributing Editor

Marion Markus
Production Assistant

Ernest L. Martin, Ph.D., FLMI
General Editor

LOMA   FLMI Insurance Education Program
Life Management Institute LOMA
Atlanta, Georgia

DON'T STOP NOW!

In FLMI Courses 1 and 2, you've learned the basics about the life and health insurance industry.

Now you can build on this knowledge by continuing your studies and earning the professional designation of Fellow, Life Management Institute.

Being an FLMI can mean being part of the leadership of the life and health insurance industry.

- ☑ 63% of FLMIs hold executive, senior management, middle management, or supervisory positions

- ☑ 33% of FLMIs earned between $50,000 and $100,000 annually in 1989

- ☑ 50% of FLMIs earned a promotion within two years of completing their designation

And FLMIs recognize the value of what they've learned. A full 87% of FLMIs reported that the FLMI Program enhanced their competence in the life and health insurance business.

Help increase your chances for professional success. Ask your Educational Representative to enroll you in the courses you need to complete your FLMI!

LOMA (Life Office Management Association, Inc.) is an international association founded in 1924. LOMA's mission is to help companies in the insurance and financial services industry improve their management and operations through quality education, research, information sharing, and related products and services. Among its activities is the sponsorship of the FLMI Insurance Education Program, an educational program intended primarily for home office and branch office employees.

The **FLMI Insurance Education Program** consists of two levels—Level I, "Fundamentals of Life and Health Insurance," and Level II, "Functional Aspects of Life and Health Insurance." Level I is designed to help students achieve a working knowledge of the life and health insurance business. Level II is designed to further the student's career development by providing a more detailed understanding of life and health insurance and related business and management subjects. Upon the completion of Level I, the student is awarded a certificate. Upon the completion of both levels, the student is designated a Fellow of the Life Management Institute (FLMI) and is awarded a diploma.

Copyright © 1992 LOMA (Life Office Management Association, Inc.)
Reprinted: July 1993

All Rights Reserved. This text, or any part thereof, may not be reproduced or transmitted in any form or by any means, electronic or mechanical, including photocopying, recording, storage in an information retrieval system, or otherwise, without the prior written permission of the publisher.

While a great deal of care has been taken to provide accurate, current, and authoritative information in regard to the subject matter covered in this book, the ideas, suggestions, general principles, conclusions, and any other information presented here are for general educational purposes only. This text is sold with the understanding that it is neither designed nor intended to provide the reader with legal, accounting, investment, marketing, or other types of professional business management advice. If legal advice or other expert assistance is required, the services of a competent professional should be sought.

ISBN 0-939921-43-X

Printed in the United States of America

Preface

This test preparation aid has been prepared for use in conjunction with *Operations of Life and Health Insurance Companies*, Second Edition, by Kenneth Huggins, FLMI/M and Robert D. Land, FLMI, ACS. It is not intended as a substitute for reading and studying this textbook. In fact, no study aid will serve as a replacement for the mental toil of absorbing the material contained in the texts; the student who attempts to abuse this test preparation aid in such a fashion will do so at his or her peril.

Neither is this publication intended as an alternative to the Student Guide published by LOMA to accompany the main textbook. The Student Guide provides an organized framework by which you can gain assistance in mastering the factual and conceptual material that is treated in the textbook. This test preparation aid, on the other hand, assumes that you have acquired the subject knowledge that comes from reading the textbooks and completing the Student Guide. It therefore makes no effort to explain the subject matter covered in those publications.

In an examination room environment, you are confronted by two obstacles. The first is represented by the limitations of your knowledge of the subject matter covered by the test. The second is your lack of familiarity with the test's format and conventions. To the extent that your lack of knowledge of the subject matter is responsible for any incorrect test responses, the test is serving its proper function as a measurement of your mastery of the assigned textual materials. However, to the extent that lack of "test-wiseness" is responsible for your failure to demonstrate attained knowledge, the test has failed to fulfill its mission. In other words, your own lack of familiarity with sound test-taking techniques may be responsible for a lower score. The goals of this publication are to (1) provide pointers to help you focus your study effort toward the final objective of taking the test, (2) provide some orientation to test-taking techniques, (3) furnish sample questions on each major text chapter so that you will have an opportunity to measure the degree of your own preparedness while simultaneously becoming more familiar with the nature of questions appearing in FLMI examinations, and (4) provide you with a full-scale practice examination that is similar in nature, design, and difficulty level to the actual examination that you will be taking.

The organization of this test-taking aid is fairly basic, consisting of

1. An introductory article that provides tips on

    a. studying with the examination in mind, and
    b. developing test-taking skills with respect to FLMI examinations;

2. A section consisting of practice questions on each chapter of the assigned text, along with answer keys and a preparedness measure for each chapter's questions; and

3. A full-scale practice test based on the assigned text, along with an answer key. The practice test contains 75 questions rather than the 100 questions you may have seen in the past, because all FLMI paper examinations except Course 9 consist of 75 questions.

This Test Preparation Guide has been developed by staff members in the Examinations Department of the Education Division. The same individuals who develop the FLMI examinations also developed the practice test, using FLMI examination guidelines.

Thanks go to Susan Conant, FLMI, CEBS, HIA, for her review of the material in this publication; and to Marion Markus, Kelly Wells, and Sharon Bibee for their patient and skilled production assistance. Special thanks are given to Ernest L. Martin, Ph.D., FLMI, for his guidance as general editor and for his authorship of the sections that guide students in test-taking methodology.

Contents

Introduction	1
Preparing for FLMI Examinations	1
Tips on Studying for an Examination	2
Secure the Right Textbooks	2
Read the Study Note in the LOMA Insurance Education Catalog	3
Focus Review Efforts by Anticipating the Examination Writer	4
How to Take an Examination	6
I*STAR or Paper Examination?	6
Becoming Test-Wise	6
Reading a Test Question	7
Answering the Easier Questions First	8
Answering the More Difficult Questions	8
Tackling the Tough Ones	8
Checking Your Answers	9
Checking Your Answer Sheet (Paper examinations only)	9
Reviewing I*STAR Answer Responses	9
Some Test-Taking Myths	9
An Overview of Question Types	10
The Applications Emphasis of Current FLMI Examinations	15
A Note on Modification of Examination Format	18
After the Examination	18
Practice Questions	21
Practice Test	69
Text References and Answer Key	86

Introduction

Students who achieve high scores on FLMI examinations do so as a result of (1) a thorough and sensibly organized study program, and (2) the use of common sense in taking the examination. This two-step approach to achieving good results on an examination would seem self-evident, and yet large numbers of otherwise intelligent students do not know how to study for an examination in the FLMI Insurance Education Program, and even larger numbers lack any kind of "test-wiseness" when confronted by an examination.

Effective study and logical test-taking involve important questions of technique, as well as of intelligence or learning ability. In the case of studying, the task consists of using the available time most efficiently to achieve maximum results. In the examination room, the task consists of using logical thought processes and a little knowledge about the nature of tests to make sure that the final score reflects fully all the knowledge that the student has attained. It is how one studies that determines the learning efficiency. Similarly, how one takes a test has a great impact on whether the final score reasonably reflects the degree of knowledge absorbed.

You should be aware of LOMA's policy concerning the use of calculators. Students may use only a calculator bearing the official LOMA seal while sitting for this examination. Student use of non-LOMA calculators will constitute a violation of regulations governing administration of FLMI examinations, and the examination will not be accepted for grading. The policy allowing only LOMA calculators into examination rooms does not affect the content or difficulty level of examinations, and calculator use is not necessary to pass any FLMI examination. Your company's educational representative will be able to assist you in securing an official LOMA calculator.

PREPARING FOR FLMI EXAMINATIONS

Unless you have many years of formal experience and schooling in the subject area covered by the examination for which you are enrolled, you will discover that there is no substitute for devoting considerable time to studying the textual materials on which the examination is based. Moreover, even those students who have the advantage of a working knowledge of an examination's subject seldom achieve very high scores without reading the assigned textual materials. The examination for which you will sit is based exclusively on the assigned textual materials; since every textbook differs in its coverage and approach in some ways from other available textbooks in the subject field, you are unlikely to achieve a high score if you do not read the assigned text(s).

Start your study program as soon as you enroll for the examination. Waiting until the last month or two before you are scheduled to sit for the examination will usually result, at best, in a marginal score. Set up a regular schedule for study, preferably including at least three study sessions per week, and establish that schedule in such a way that you have completed the first reading of the assigned textual materials at least two months before the date of the examination.

Not all students benefit from the same studying techniques. One technique or studying process that seems to work for many students is the comprehensive, staged approach.

Under this approach, once you have completed the initial reading of the textual materials, use the Student Guide(s) while working through the text(s) again. Only after you complete that process should you turn to this publication, working carefully through the practice questions from each chapter of the assigned textual materials and finally taking the complete practice test appearing at the end.

Alternatively, some students find the chapter-by-chapter approach more beneficial. In this approach, you read one chapter at a time, then proceed to work through the Student Guide and finally through the practice questions for the chapter in this publication. Again, your reading of chapters should be sequential — in their proper order.

Your study schedule should allow two to three weeks for a final review, and during that period you should use to your advantage some of the tips given here to make the most of your final review time.

There are some study practices to avoid at all costs. Don't delay in beginning your study schedule to the point that you are forced to skip the final chapters of the text(s). Remember that the test will cover all chapters that are assigned. Let's say that the final three chapters of an assigned text account for, on average, twelve points in the typical 100-point test. If you do not allow enough time to read and study these chapters, the chances are that you are starting to take the test with a maximum potential score of only 88, leaving yourself with a margin for error of only 18, rather than the standard 30, points.

Read the chapters sequentially. Information needed for a complete understanding of later chapters will generally be provided in preceding chapters. Don't handicap yourself with a hit-and-miss approach to absorbing the large amount of material.

Finally, avoid reliance on old examinations as study aids. There are two very good reasons to do so. First, assigned textual materials for FLMI courses change considerably more frequently today than in the past. Such changes are part of an effort to keep FLMI study assignments more current. Thus, the old examination you rely upon may be based on a text no longer assigned. Secondly, test-building methodology in the FLMI Insurance Education Program has changed considerably in recent cycles. Old tests are no longer reliable guides to what you can expect to encounter in the testing room; in fact, the student who relies on old tests to measure preparedness for a current examination is likely to encounter a rather disagreeable surprise at actual test time. This is one reason that LOMA no longer makes old tests available to students. The full-scale practice test at the end of this publication reflects test-building methodology currently in use. It is a much better indicator of your level of preparedness than any of the old FLMI tests you might otherwise use in the study process.

TIPS ON STUDYING FOR AN EXAMINATION

Secure the Right Textbooks

There is hardly a sadder circumstance than the one that some FLMI students encounter when they discover — too late — that they have studied from the wrong textbook(s). It happens more often than you might think. No matter how diligently you have studied, the Education Division cannot make allowances for such a mistake — even if someone else in your company made the mistake. The required textual materials for each course in the FLMI curriculum are listed in the LOMA Insurance Education Catalog; there will be no departure from this listing. The Education Catalog clearly specifies that it is the student's responsibility to acquire the proper textbooks and to study them.

Normally, your company's educational representative is assigned the task of ordering and distributing textbooks for enrolled students. However, keep in mind that it is your responsibility to check the textbooks against the listing in the current Education Catalog. (Make sure that you use the Education Catalog for the year in which you plan to sit for the examination.) When you receive your textbook(s), check each one against the Education Catalog listing. If there have been multiple editions of an assigned textbook, be sure that you have the edition that will be used for testing purposes. Do not assume that the second edition of a text will do just as well if the third edition is the assigned text. In almost all cases, there are very substantial changes between editions of a textbook used in the FLMI Insurance Education Program. In fact, the Education Division at LOMA takes extraordinary steps to guard against adopting or publishing texts which represent only very minor editorial changes from previous editions in use.

The Education Catalog lists all textual materials that will be required under the heading "Assigned Texts." Sometimes, the assignments for Canadian students will be different from those for United States students. Check the Education Catalog listing to be sure that you are reading the assigned text listing for your own country.

Another listing of textual materials comes under the heading "Suggested Study Aids." For the most part, these study aids are designed to assist the student in preparing for an examination; these materials consist of student guides, pretests, or background reading. The suggested study aids would not be listed if they had not been determined to be helpful to the student. However, they are optional and not required. By themselves, they will not be part of the materials from which questions on the test will be drawn. The assigned text(s), on the other hand, will be tested over in detail. It will be essential to your success on the examination for you to read the assigned text(s) thoroughly.

While you are reading the listing under the heading "Assigned Texts" in your Education Catalog note carefully those texts which are preceded by a double check mark. A double check mark by the title indicates that a new and different textbook has been placed in use for the first time. The existence of such check marks calls for you to check the textbooks that you have acquired to be sure that they correspond with the current listing.

If your company maintains a library of FLMI textbooks, be sure that the textbooks in stock are the correct titles and editions. Your educational representative and/or your company librarian will make every effort to maintain a current supply of textbooks. However, in case you were to select the wrong textbooks from the shelves, the consequences to your chances of success on the examination could be serious. Whatever the reason for your securing the wrong textbooks, it is important for you to remember that you will not be relieved of responsibility for acquiring the correct textbooks merely because you found them on a library shelf. The responsibility for securing the proper textbooks as you begin your study is yours and yours alone. This fact would be true even in the unlikely event that someone in your company supplied you with out-of-date textbooks.

Read the Study Note in the LOMA Insurance Education Catalog

In cases in which a course in the FLMI curriculum has multiple assigned textbooks, the LOMA Insurance Education Catalog will begin the course description with a study note. This study note will contain the recommendations of the Education Division with respect to a desirable sequence, if any, in which the assigned textbooks are to be read. It will give an indication of the percentage range of test questions that will be drawn from each textbook or broad subject category — an important and reliable clue as to how many questions will be drawn from a given textbook. Finally, the study note will indicate any special characteristics of examination format — whether there are separate sections or examinations for the United States and the Canadian assignments, for example.

Focus Review Efforts by Anticipating the Examination Writer

A test is a sample of knowledge. Not every concept presented in an FLMI curriculum assignment can be the subject of testing. Limitations of space and testing time require that an examination author choose the material to be used as a sample of a student's knowledge with great care. The FLMI Insurance Education Program also places great emphasis on fairness to the student body by avoiding such practices as ambiguous wording and selection of extremely minor material for testing.

You can be certain that the fundamentals of a course will be covered in every course examination — that is, concepts basic to an understanding of the subject will always be selected for testing, although the approach or the type of question used for the testing will likely differ every time. After those basic concepts have been covered, the examination author is free to choose the remainder of "optional" concepts to be selected. The material which follows is designed to help you anticipate what optional concepts are likely to be eligible for selection.

The time that remains before you sit for your examination will dictate the extent of your final review of the assigned textual materials. Ideally, you would have read and reread all assigned materials, working through the Student Guide(s) as you did so. Suppose, however, that you had very little time remaining for your final review of the textual materials before you were to take the test. Fortunately, in such a case, you can maximize the payoff from your review by anticipating what textual material is a sure-fire bet to be tested and, on the other hand, what material is highly unlikely to be the subject of a substantial number of questions on the test.

The professionals in the Education Division who devote their full-time efforts to developing the examinations used in the FLMI Insurance Education Program work according to certain test-writing ground rules. All of these rules are directed toward ensuring maximum fairness to the student. An example of a ground rule applied in the test development process is the one which dictates that all material selected for testing appear in the assigned textbook(s) and also be current with actual practice within the life insurance industry. If the material does not meet both of these criteria, it will not be covered by a test question. Furthermore, if somehow a question based on invalid material were to appear in a test and were to be challenged by students or instructors, it would be invalidated — all students would receive credit for the question. Other such rules apply specifically to the selection of textual material on which test questions will be based.

Knowing some of these rules will help you to determine what textual material is absolutely essential for you to know before sitting for the examination and, on the other hand, what material you might give only a minimal review.

Each rule discussed in the following pages will first be quoted directly from the training manual used by examination writers at LOMA. The implications of the rule will then be discussed.

Rule 1: An item should not be based solely on an author's opinion.

Keeping this rule in mind while you attempt to anticipate what material will be the basis for test questions will help you eliminate some possibly informative but untestable material. In actual practice, the personnel who develop the FLMI examinations avoid basing test questions on material that is unique to the textbook author — that is, material that presents theories or interprets facts in a fashion that is contrary to the dominant accepted opinion in the academic community of scholars who have expertise in the subject area. Moreover, even if such theories or facts are consistent with those held by the academic community at large, they will not be subject to testing if they are presented as authorial opinion rather than theory or fact.

Although the Education Division strives to develop and to select textual materials that reflect mainstream thinking, some commercially available textbooks contain some passages that reflect authorial opinion or bias.

Whereas you should read the entire textbook, you can eliminate some material for your final review by marking passages that clearly represent authorial opinion as you are undertaking your initial reading.

Rule 2: Textual material selected for testing should emphasize facts and current industry practices. Therefore, an examination writer should de-emphasize historical or prospectively oriented material.

To illustrate material that is likely to receive less emphasis according to this rule, let's examine the following passage:

> One of the more interesting of the computer pioneers was Charles Babbage. Like many of his predecessors, Babbage dreamed of a machine to compute and print mathematical tables and, in 1823, started work on just such a machine, his difference engine. With some support from the British government, Babbage began to design his difference engine, actually beginning construction in 1830. During the planning stages, however, he expanded his view of the problem and envisioned another machine, an analytical engine, which would be capable of solving more general problems. By 1834, Babbage had abandoned plans for his difference engine and began devoting his full energy to the analytical engine. (William S. Davis, *Computers and Business Information Processing*, pp. 73-74.)

Several textbooks used in the FLMI Insurance Education Program contain limited amounts of historical material. In your final review, you can spare yourself some time by emphasizing such material less. The general concept of such material is more important than is learning specific dates, for example. The final test of the suitability of such material for testing is whether the material provides background necessary for an understanding of subsequent concepts.

Some texts also conclude with a forward look at likely developments in the industry or in a subject area. Such glances at the future, while very interesting, lack much of the factual basis that renders them subject to extensive testing. This statement should not be construed to mean, however, that a test question or two based on such material might not appear on an examination.

Rule 3: An item should not be based on trivial material, or on material found exclusively in a footnote.

The material on which FLMI test questions are based is to be found in the main body of the text. Keep in mind, however, that a text glossary, if part of an assigned textbook, is not regarded as trivial material. For test-writing purposes, footnotes are considered to be supplementary and thus secondary to the main text.

You should not, however, regard charts and graphs presented within an assigned textbook as trivial material. In many cases, authors choose charts and graphs as a primary means of conveying knowledge. The emphasis of FLMI examinations in testing material found in charts and graphs will be primarily on the main concepts such vehicles convey, rather than on requiring you to memorize dates, brands of equipment, etc.

These are the three principal examination development rules that you should keep in mind in distinguishing between testable and untestable textual material for review purposes. There are, however, two more which, taken together, can provide you with valuable clues as to what material is susceptible to testing:

Rule 4: An item should not be based on a textual passage that is contradicted by other assigned study material.

Rule 4 is designed to protect the student from having to choose between contradictory statements within a textbook or between two textbooks; in instances where contradictions occur, the examination writer is obliged to ignore the material directly affected by the contradictory passage.

Rule 5: An item that has a United States context, rather than a context which includes Canada, and vice versa, should specify that context clearly in the introductory section of the item.

Rule 5 addresses the matter of testing on practices that differ between the United States and Canada. In general, where a question addresses specifically the practices in only one country, it must specify that the question is concerned with only the one country. The important implication here is that, unless an examination contains a Canadian section and a United States section from which the student is to choose, there will be a limit to the number of test questions that are specific to only one country. In practice, this limit is three to five questions per examination. Moreover, fairness dictates that there be a roughly equal number of questions within an examination that are devoted to each country's practices; for instance, no test will contain ten questions that address only United States practices, and a mere two questions addressing Canadian practices. Keep this rule in mind when you are reviewing. In analyzing sections on Canadian practices, focus on the differences between United States and Canadian practices. Practices that are common to the two countries will be addressed in the more general textual treatments of topics.

Finally, with all the rules in mind, anticipate the thought processes of the examination writer by analyzing textual passages to see whether you could construct a test question on the material by using the four question formats that are treated in the following section of this introduction. If you believe that you could do so fairly easily, then there is a good chance that the material lends itself well to testing and therefore should be included in your final review. If you find otherwise, then chances are that the examination writer would also encounter trouble in basing a question on the material while still following the rules. If you are uncertain as to the material's testability, play it safe and include the material in your final review.

HOW TO TAKE AN EXAMINATION

I*STAR or Paper Examination?

The first eight courses in the FLMI Insurance Education Program are available in two forms — by computer and on paper.

I*STAR, LOMA's examination-by-computer system, is available in the United States, Canada, and other countries via LOMANET, LOMA's telecommunications network.

Students in the many companies that have installed I*STAR facilities enjoy the convenience of sitting for examinations at any time of the year, without regard to the strict administration schedule which governs paper examinations. There is no pre-registration period for I*STAR examinations. In fact, students enroll for and take an I*STAR examination at the same sitting. Companies are billed for examinations administered. I*STAR students receive on-screen notification of examination results immediately upon completion of an examination.

Of course, all FLMI courses continue to be available in paper form. Many of these courses are available twice per year. Students must be enrolled and fees paid well in advance of the scheduled examination administration, and the examination administration schedule published in the LOMA Insurance Education Catalog must be strictly adhered to. Students normally receive examination results four to six weeks after sitting for FLMI Program examinations.

While paper examinations generally contain 75 questions, I*STAR examinations may contain either 75 or 100 questions. However, regardless of whether a student sits for I*STAR or paper examinations, the construction and difficulty of the examinations will be comparable.

The material which follows applies to either type of examination.

Becoming Test-Wise

Some individuals seem to have a special knack for taking an examination, whereas others leave the examination room feeling frustrated that the test itself, rather than ignorance of the subject matter on which the examination is based, has been a major obstacle. It is important to recognize, however, that "test-wise" individuals possess no magical talent, but instead use a combination of common sense and logic to enhance their chances of answering questions correctly, even when they have little or no knowledge of the subject matter on which such questions are based. Unfortunately, too many students leave common sense and logic behind them when they enter a room where an examination is to be administered; anxious and somewhat rattled by the stress that is common to the test-taking environment, such students make foolish mistakes or play against the odds in answering test questions. The result is a loss of valuable or even essential points that sometimes spell the difference between success and failure on the examination.

There is no special talent involved in becoming a test-wise student. If you will develop a methodology — a systematic and logical way of approaching a test — you can become adept at test-taking. Of course, there is no substitute for adequate test preparation; no matter how excellent your test-taking skills, you will not be successful on an FLMI examination merely by adopting a logical system of guessing the correct answers. Experts, including college professors, who have been involved in reviewing the examinations for soundness have tried, without notable success, to use guessing without the aid of subject knowledge. Nevertheless, there are techniques that you can use to avoid defeating yourself through making test-taking mistakes.

Reading a Test Question

Take, for example, the approach to reading a test question. Too many students read each question as though there were a fire in the building where the examination was being administered. However, in each test, some questions require especially careful reading, lest an incorrect response be unintentionally chosen. The following question illustrates the point:

Jane Welch purchased a life insurance policy in the United States and named Bob Myers, her father, as the party to receive the proceeds upon her death. Ms. Welch agreed to give up her right to change this beneficiary designation. In this situation, Mr. Myers is the

(1) contingent, revocable beneficiary
(2) contingent, irrevocable beneficiary
(3) primary, revocable beneficiary
(4) primary, irrevocable beneficiary

Too often, the hurried approach leads one to choose immediately the answer that incompletely answers the question: in this case, hurry will lead the student to focus on whether the father is the contingent or the primary beneficiary. Since answer choice (3) is the first one to satisfy the requirement that the beneficiary be primary, you would expect that many students who are working hurriedly would choose it — and the test results would prove you right. However, the correct answer should satisfy two requirements listed in the question's introduction: that the beneficiary be primary, and also that the beneficiary be irrevocable. The correct response is answer choice (4), but unfortunately too many rapid-fire students never get beyond answer choice (3). The result is that test points are forfeited — not because the student lacked the requisite knowledge to answer the question correctly, but because of a fault in the test-taking methodology.

A related mistake occurs when one fails to read the question's "stem," or introduction, correctly because of hurry. Take, for example, the following question:

An insurance company incorporated under the laws of the state of New York is also domiciled in New York and maintains the majority of its business in New York. From the point of view of any other state in the United States, such an insurance company is considered to be

(1) a foreign corporation
(2) a domestic corporation
(3) an alien corporation
(4) a closed corporation

It is surprising to discover how many students incorrectly chose answer (2) for this question — not because they do not know the difference between a foreign and a domestic corporation (the only two really credible choices), but because they failed to read the question's stem carefully. Apparently the large number of students who chose answer (2) read the introductory sentence, determined that it effectively defined a domestic corporation from the point of view of New York, and gave little attention at all to the lead-in sentence, which asked that the insurance company be considered from the point of view of "any other state." Thus, we come to the first rule in our test-taking methodology:

(1) Read the entire question before attempting to answer it, and recognize the key concepts in the stem.

By key concepts, we refer to those elements in the question's introduction that are crucial to the nature of the question. In this case, key concepts would include "insurance company," "incorporated under the laws of New York," "domiciled in New York," and "maintains the majority of its business in New York." The concept that would require double-underlining would be "From the point of view of any other state," for this phrase is essential for answering the question correctly.

Answering the Easier Questions First

Another sound practice in taking any examination is to answer first only those questions of which you are absolutely certain, leaving until later those questions about which you have any doubt. Work completely through the test, entering your responses to the easier questions. In this way, you will later be able to focus exclusively on those questions that require a greater degree of thought. Thus,

(2) Work completely through the test, answering only those questions of which you are absolutely certain.

If you are sitting for a paper examination, you should keep a record of your responses by entering the responses you choose next to the corresponding question numbers in your question leaflet. If you are sitting for an I*STAR examination, use the Recall option to mark questions of which you are uncertain. A menu option permits you to review and reconsider all questions on the Recall list.

Answering the More Difficult Questions

Once you have completed the questions that you found easiest to answer, you will be ready to give consideration to those questions about which you have greater doubt. Some of these will be easier than others. During this second round, answer only those remaining questions that you are able, with reasonable certainty, to work out the answers to. Therefore,

(3) Go through the test a second time and answer the questions that you can answer with reasonable certainty.

Tackling the Tough Ones

Now you are ready to deal with those questions that are proving to be the most difficult to you. Go back through the test and answer all questions that you have left unanswered. If you can eliminate some responses, do so and focus only on those answer choices which you have not ruled out.

If you have no idea of the correct answer to a question, take an educated guess. Remember, the only part of the test that will be subjected to the grading process is your answer sheet. If you do not provide an answer to a question, it will automatically be marked incorrect; on the other hand, your educated guesses on the questions that you are unsure of have a chance of being correct. In a later section on the various types of question formats utilized in FLMI examinations, you will be given some tips on how to use the process of elimination and some knowledge of test-writing practices in the FLMI Program to improve your chances of guessing correctly. Again, keep a record of your responses in your question leaflet.

(4) Go through the entire test a third time, providing answers to each previously unanswered question. If you can eliminate some answer

choices for a question, do so. If necessary, provide a sensible guess for questions of which you are uncertain.

Checking Your Answers

Once you have provided an answer to every question, go back through the entire examination and reconsider your answers. Be cautious in making changes, unless it is clear that you made a mistake in providing an answer. In cases where you had to guess, usually your first guess is the best one. It is surprising to discover how many times students remove a correct answer choice and enter an incorrect one during this phase. Use caution in making changes; change your original answer choice only if you are certain that you made a mistake in choosing it.

Checking Your Answer Sheet (Paper examinations only)

In addition, check the entries that you have made on your answer sheet. Remember, the only part of the test that will be subjected to the grading process is your answer sheet. If you have recorded your answers improperly, there will be no extra consideration given to your answer sheet. In fact, the staff of the Education Division cannot make any changes in the answer sheets once they have been delivered. One of the most common errors made by students is misalignment of answer sheet spaces — a student intending to answer question 6 uses the answer sheet space for question 7 to record the answer, for example, and ever afterwards the mistake is compounded. You can ensure against making such a mistake by using a folded sheet of paper to check each line of the answer sheet against the responses that you have recorded in your question leaflet. In this way, you will both ensure that your answer sheet entries have been made properly and also check for any discrepancies between the answers that you recorded on your question leaflet and the entries that you made on the answer sheet.

Reviewing I*STAR Answer Responses

If you are sitting for an I*STAR examination, use the menu option which permits you to go back through the examination, and make certain that the answer responses are the ones you intended to enter.

*(5) Go back through the test and reconsider every answer choice, making any changes with caution. Then check the answer sheet against the recorded answers in your question leaflet. For I*STAR examinations, make sure all recorded responses are the ones you intended.*

Following these five steps in the test-taking methodology should help you become test-wise. In the next subsection, we will examine some test-taking myths, and then we will look at the various question formats that you will encounter when you sit for an FLMI examination.

Some Test-Taking Myths

No matter how diligently you prepare for the examination, you will be handicapped if you adhere to some test-taking myths that circulate through groups of students with almost self-perpetuating force. Here are a few:

Myth 1: Answer choice (1) is the best choice if it is necessary to guess the correct answer to a question, because test-makers usually place the correct answer first.

Fact: The correct answers to the questions appearing on an FLMI examination are evenly balanced among choices (1), (2), (3), and (4). So rigidly is this principle adhered to that the examination specialists routinely prepare a correct answer number distribution chart as part of the final editing process, so as to avoid developing such a habit as is suggested by the myth.

Myth 2: There is usually a pattern to the answer key responses.

Fact: There is no pattern to the order of the numerical responses to the questions in an FLMI examination except that the distribution of correct numerical responses be evenly balanced, or relatively so.

Myth 3: Always choose the longest response to a question, because examination writers are careful to qualify the correct answer more than they qualify the incorrect answers.

Fact: Because the examination specialists at LOMA are especially alert to this tendency in examinations in some other testing programs, they take special care to avoid such a pattern. In fact, the shortest answer is as likely to be correct, and average-length answers may be even more likely than the longest answer. Part of the standard training for an examination writer is in varying the length of the correct answer response so as to avoid tipping off the student to the correct answer.

An Overview of Question Types

In the FLMI examinations, a limited number of basic question formats are used extensively. The majority of the questions that you encounter will take one of these formats or variations thereof. Knowing something about the nature of these question types can help you in anticipating the nature of the test and in providing educated guesses in cases in which you are unsure of the correct answer. Read the following subsection with care so that you become thoroughly familiar with the question types and so that you can develop some sensible test-taking habits in approaching them.

The question types utilized by the test developers for the FLMI Insurance Education Program have been proven through many years of experience to produce sound results without at the same time confusing the student unnecessarily. These question types include (1) the straightforward multiple-choice question, consisting of an introduction (called a "stem") and four answer choices; (2) the multiple-statement question, consisting of a stem and a series of responses, the student's objective being to select the proper grouping of responses; (3) the matching question, consisting of a series of items in one column that is to be matched with another series of responses in a second column; and (4) the two-statement combination question, an adaptation of the multiple-statement question.

Typically, the straightforward multiple-choice questions will make up about 70 to 90 percent of an examination.

1. The Straightforward Multiple-Choice Question

The question reprinted below is representative of the straightforward multiple-choice type of question:

If the premiums for an employer-employee group life insurance contract are paid entirely by the employer, the group insurance plan is said to be

(1) coinsured
(2) vested
(3) nonfunded
(4) non-contributory

A little common sense and the process of elimination will considerably improve your chances of choosing the correct response. First of all, reading the question's stem carefully will allow you to extract the key concepts covered by the question. In this case, the key concepts are (1) premium payments, (2) employer-employee group life insurance, and (3) premium payments made solely by the employer. The correct answer choice, therefore, applies to a situation in which the employer pays 100 percent of the premium for a group life insurance plan and the employees pay none.

Now you can use the process of elimination and your knowledge of life insurance terminology to eliminate the incorrect answer choices. First of all, you can eliminate *coinsured* as a possible response. This term has nothing to do with premium payments or group life insurance, but instead describes a situation in which the insured under a *health* insurance contract pays a specified percentage of eligible expenses of a claim. Notice that you have used the *key concepts* in the question's stem to eliminate this answer choice. The second choice, *vested*, is so general that it cannot possibly apply to premium payments. It is one of those terms designed to look attractive to the student who has not bothered to read the textbook. The third answer choice, *nonfunded*, is unrelated to either premium payments or group life insurance. It represents terminology that relates to a *pension* plan's funds.

The process of elimination has therefore left only one answer choice, (4) non-contributory. This term properly describes a situation in which the employees covered by a group life insurance plan make no contributions to premium payments.

Consider another example of the straightforward multiple-choice question:

> In a life insurance company that is departmentalized on a product basis, one example of a product division is the
>
> (1) legal department
> (2) accounting department
> (3) group department
> (4) underwriting department

Here, the key concepts in the stem are (1) life insurance company, (2) departmentalization on a product basis, and (3) product division. The task is to determine which of the answer choices exemplifies a product division in a life insurance company. Certainly choice (1) can be eliminated, since a legal department is not directly related to a life insurance product, although the legal department would certainly perform tasks associated with product development and administration. The same would be true for choice (2), since an accounting department would be connected more with administrative aspects of a company than with a product line, and for choice (4), which represents an activity rather than a product. The remaining choice is (3), which is correct because group insurance is a product of a life insurance company.

2. The Multiple-Statement Question Type

Multiple-statement questions generally have the highest level of difficulty of all the question types, since they cover a wider range of textual materials and require both individual and collective evaluation of answer choices. They need not, however, be any more difficult than other types.

One important approach that is useful in responding to multiple-statement questions is to extract key concepts from the question's stem and then to use the process of elimination in narrowing the possible answer combinations.

Consider, for example, the following multiple-statement question:

> An applicant for life insurance usually has a choice with respect to some of the provisions and privileges that will be included in the policy. Typically, the applicant has a choice as to
>
> A. How frequently premiums are to be paid
> B. Whether a reinstatement privilege is to be included
> C. How policy dividends, if any, are to be used or applied
> D. To whom policy proceeds are to be paid
>
> (1) All of these
> (2) A, C and D only
> (3) B, C and D only
> (4) A and B only
> (5) C and D only

Key concepts in the question stem are (1) life insurance, (2) the applicant's ability to choose, and (3) policy provisions and privileges. The question calls for the student to determine which of the listed provisions and privileges are a matter of the applicant's choosing when a life insurance policy is applied for.

Typically, the applicant for life insurance has a choice of how frequently premiums are to be paid; therefore, *A* is definitely true. Any of the numbered groupings that do not contain *A* are incorrect responses. Immediately, the student, by knowing *A* is true, can eliminate groupings (3) and (5), which do not contain *A*, thereby improving the odds of choosing the correct response from one in five to one in three.

Now consider statement *B*. An applicant does not have a choice of whether a reinstatement provision will be included in a life insurance policy. Although all of Canada and about half the states require that a reinstatement provision be included by a company in a policy contract, the individual has no choice in the matter. Knowing that *B* is false not only allows the student to doubly eliminate grouping (3), but also to eliminate groupings (1) and (4), which contain *B*.

Through knowing that *A* is true and *B* is false, the student has used the process of elimination to eliminate choices (1), (3), (4), and (5). There is only one choice remaining — (2) — and it is the correct answer.

Even if you were unable to evaluate *both A* and *B*, but you were sure that *one* of them was correct or incorrect, the continued use of the process of elimination for *C* and *D* would greatly improve your chances of answering correctly.

Consider another example of a multiple-statement question:

> A minor is held responsible for the fair value of his or her contracts for necessaries. The term *necessaries* is ordinarily held to include
>
> A. Food
> B. Entertainment
> C. Shelter
> D. Transportation
>
> (1) All of these
> (2) A, B and D only
> (3) A, C and D only
> (4) A and C only
> (5) B and C only

Let's say that you had time only to skim the chapter on which this question is based and that you are going to have to make an educated guess. The process of elimination can still be helpful. First of all, a common sense evaluation of the term *necessaries* as it applies to minors is likely to indicate that entertainment (*B*) is least likely to be absolutely necessary for a child. On the other hand, food and shelter (*A* and *C*) are essential for survival. Even your hunch about these three terms and the vaguest notion of the term *necessary* can lead to the choice of the correct answer. Elimination of any grouping containing *B* removes (1), (2), and (5) from consideration, since they all contain *B*. You are now left with (3) and (4) to evaluate. The difference between them is that (3) contains *D*, whereas (4) does not.

You now need to evaluate only *D* to determine the correct answer grouping. Even if you have no idea of whether transportation is a necessary, you have used the process of elimination to give yourself a 50 percent chance of guessing correctly. A sounder strategy, however, is to consider transportation in the context of essentials, just as you did when you eliminated *B*. Such an evaluation of *D* would likely indicate that although transportation is certainly important, it is hardly essential in all circumstances. Moreover, since the stem of the question specifically mentions necessaries with respect to minors, it is hardly likely that a minor would need to own a car or other mode of transportation. Common sense and a very broad concept of the meaning of the word *necessary* would indicate that *D* is not "ordinarily" a necessary. Elimination of *D* leaves only grouping (4), which is the correct answer.

Even if you are unable to evaluate all the items or statements under *A*, *B*, *C*, etc., even knowing one can improve your chances of guessing correctly — and remember that there is no extra penalty for incorrect guessing.

Finally, if common sense and the process of elimination fail to narrow your choices (say you are completely unable to evaluate any statement), use a little knowledge about examination development practices to aid you in guessing. An examination writer sometimes includes the statement he or she considers most likely to be guessed as true in several groupings. Conversely, the statement that the examination writer considers as most likely to be perceived as false tends to be included in only one or two of the groupings. With this examination development tendency in mind, see if you can evaluate the following question to determine which statements are most likely and least likely to be true:

According to Rensis Likert's organizational profiles, an organization that is categorized as a "System 4" organization has the following characteristics:

A. Primary emphasis of the control processes is on blame setting rather than problem solving
B. Subordinates feel free to discuss with their superiors the problems that the subordinates encounter on the job
C. Superiors recognize the importance of training in the development of their subordinates
D. Control processes are dispersed throughout the organization

(1) All of these
(2) A, B and C only
(3) B, C and D only
(4) B and D only
(5) C and D only

The statements appearing most frequently in the groupings are B, C, and D — four times each. One possibility is to eliminate all groupings that do not contain all of these statements — in this case, (5) does not contain B and (4) does not contain C, while (2) does not contain D. This sheer guessing strategy has left you with two groupings still to be considered — (1) and (3). Now consider the statement that is used least frequently — A, which is used only twice. According to this guessing strategy, you would eliminate (1), which contains A. You are left with only (3), which happens to be the correct answer.

Ready for another exercise in test-wiseness? Try this one without evaluating the truth or falseness of the statements, but only by determining the most-used and least-used statements:

Typical sources of life insurance company investment income include

A. Rent collected on real estate owned
B. Increases in policy reserves
C. Interest received on policy loans
D. Interest received on mortgage loans

(1) A, B and D only
(2) A, C and D only
(3) B, C and D only
(4) A and C only
(5) A and D only

First of all, you should prepare a listing of the frequency of appearance of each letter in the groupings, as follows:

Letter	Times Used
A	4
B	2
C	3
D	4

Obviously, B is the least-used letter. Therefore, guessing strategy would indicate that all groupings containing B should be eliminated — in this question, (1) and (3). Similarly, only groupings containing A and D should be considered, thus eliminating in addition (4), which does not contain D. You are now left with only (2) and (5) to consider. Since analysis indicates that C is used in the groupings three times — almost as many times as A and D — C is likely to be true. The only one of the two remaining statements that uses A and D as well as C is (2), which happens to be the correct answer.

This guessing strategy should be used only when all else fails. It will not always work. Examination writers are by aptitude and training capable of anticipating likely student responses and of breaking predictable patterns occasionally. At best, the most-used, least-used approach to guessing the correct response to multiple-statement items should be utilized as you would use a fire extinguisher — only in emergencies.

3. The Matching Question Type

Matching questions as used in FLMI examinations are characterized generally by coverage of a relatively large amount of textual material. It is not uncommon for a series of matching questions to be drawn from thematically related material appearing in four or five textbook chapters. Typical matching questions are illustrated below. Usually, as in this series, answer choices exceed the number of questions by 50 percent.

You should keep in mind that unless the directions for the series of matching questions specify otherwise, each answer choice is used only once. Therefore, it is possible to use the process of elimination to improve your chances of answering correctly. For example, suppose you are certain that the answer to question 57 is (6) and that the answer to question 60 is (4). In attempting to answer questions 58 and 59, you are left with only four of the original answer choices, since (4) and (6) have already been used. If you should decide that the answer to question 58 is (1), then you are left with only three possible answer choices — (2), (3), and (5) — for question 59.

Again, careful attention to recognizing key concepts in each question and using common sense is infinitely preferable to sheer guessing.

If, however, you are reduced to guessing, pay particular attention to the directions for the matching series. Sometimes these directions will conclude with the statement, "Answer choices may be used more than once or not at all." If this statement appears in the directions, it is a good bet that at least one of the answer choices will be correct for two questions, and all bets for using the process of elimination are off. The multiple use of one answer choice in a series of matching questions has become a more pronounced trend recently in the FLMI examinations.

4. The Two-Statement Combination Question Type

A typical two-statement combination question is as follows:

> After paying the premiums on his non-participating whole life insurance policy for 5 years, Paul Shillin wishes to discontinue premium payments. In this situation, the following nonforfeiture option(s) are available to Mr. Shillin:

Questions 57 through 60 are matching questions. In the left-hand column are terms associated with the study of jobs. Alongside the corresponding question number on your Answer Sheet, fill in the space containing the number of the statement in the right-hand column that best describes each term.

57. Job enlargement

58. Job analysis

59. Job evaluation

60. Job enrichment

(1) A method for identifying the important dimensions of a job that help distinguish it from other jobs

(2) The relative complexity of an assigned task as reflected by its cycle time

(3) Attaching a dollar value to a job so that jobs can be compared on the basis of value

(4) Building into a job greater scope for personal achievement, recognition, and responsibility

(5) The relative freedom that a jobholder has in planning and controlling assigned tasks

(6) Increasing the number of tasks performed by an employee

Typical matching questions

A. He can collect the cash value of the policy

B. He can collect the face amount of the policy in cash

   (1) Both A and B
   (2) A only
   (3) B only
   (4) Neither A nor B

Because there are only four possible answer choices for a two-statement combination question, the answer choice groupings for all such questions are uniform.

The use of the process of elimination for any one of the statements improves your odds of answering correctly by 50 percent. For example, suppose that you are certain that statement *A* is correct, but that you are uncertain about statement *B*. In such a case, you would be left with only (1) and (2) to consider, and your odds of guessing correctly are 50 percent. On the other hand, suppose that you are certain that statement *B* is false, but that you are uncertain about statement *A*. In this situation, you would be left with only (2) and (4) to consider, since you have effectively eliminated (1) and (3). Again, your odds of guessing correctly are improved to 50 percent.

The two-statement combination item provides better odds than any of the other question types. To illustrate, suppose you are confronted by a straightforward multiple-choice question with four answer choices, a four-statement combination question with five answer groupings, a matching series of four multiple-choice questions with six answer choices that are to be used only once, and a two-statement combination question. Further suppose that you are able to eliminate as incorrect one answer choice from each of these four questions. For the straightforward multiple-choice question, your odds of guessing the correct answer would become one in three; for the four-statement combination question, one in four; for the second matching question, one in five; but for the two-statement combination item, one in two!

THE APPLICATIONS EMPHASIS OF CURRENT FLMI EXAMINATIONS

A previous section of this publication cautioned against over-reliance on old examinations as study aids. One reason for avoiding putting too much stock in old examinations is the fact that the entire test-building methodology of FLMI examinations changes periodically.

The current emphasis of FLMI examinations is on putting the student in a decision-making role. In other words, students should be able to demonstrate that they are able to make functional use of the concepts learned. With much greater frequency than in the past, FLMI examinations require students to apply concepts to situations, rather than merely to recognize a definition of a concept. This new emphasis places a premium on a student's acquiring a functional knowledge of course concepts. For instance, instead of testing whether a student can recognize a description of the concept of present value, today's FLMI examination is much more likely to determine whether the student can calculate the present value of a sum.

The examples of questions given in the section of this guide entitled "An Overview of Question Types" are typical of the recognition or definitional type of examination question — questions that test rote memorization or general knowledge of concepts. FLMI examination specialists are now giving increased emphasis to application types of examination questions — questions that ask you to manipulate information in such a way as to put into practice a concept that has been covered by the textual materials. In other words, application questions require you to put the knowledge you have gained to work in (1) predicting the consequences of a set of facts, (2) dealing with a real-life situation, or (3) solving a problem. Application questions, therefore, call for a higher level of conceptual skill than mere recognition of a concept, term, or formula.

In order to highlight the differences between application and recognition questions, consider the following two recognition questions:

> Mark Hagel placed $100 in an investment that is guaranteed to pay 10 percent interest, compounded semiannually. At the end of two years, the value of Mr. Hagel's investment could correctly be calculated using the formula
>
> (1) $100 \times (1.05)^2$
> (2) $100 \times (1.10)^2$
> (3) $100 \times (1.05)^4$
> (4) $100 \times (1.10)^4$

This question merely requires that you be able to correctly recognize the formula for the future value of a sum of money, given semiannual interest payments. It does not require you to manipulate the data, or apply any knowledge toward actually solving the problem. The correct answer here is choice (3), because over a two-year period there will be four semiannual payments of five percent (one-half of ten percent) each.

> Tables of present value and future value interest factors can greatly simplify a calculation of the time value of money. If, in a time value calculation, the time period equals 15 years and the correct interest factor equals 0.362, then the calculation must involve the determination of the
>
> (1) future value of a single sum of money
> (2) future value of an annuity
> (3) present value of a single sum of money
> (4) present value of an annuity

This question also requires no manipulation of information — so it is not an application question — but it does require a higher level of recognition on your part than the first example.

Questions requiring higher levels of recognition are becoming more common on all FLMI examinations. The correct answer here is choice (3), since all present value interest factors for single sums of money are less than or equal to one. All interest factors related to answer choices (1), (2), and (4) are greater than or equal to one when the time period involved is greater than one year (or one period if the time frame is expressed in units other than years).

By contrast, consider the following application question:

> Mark Hagel placed $100 in an investment that is guaranteed to pay 10 percent interest, compounded semiannually. At the end of two years, Mr. Hagel's investment will be worth
>
> (1) $110.25
> (2) $121.00
> (3) $121.55
> (4) $146.41

This question is the same as the first example given above, except that rather than giving you formulas as the answer choices, the question gives you the results of the calculations using those formulas. This change converts the question to an application question, since it requires you to apply an ungiven formula to a given set of data in order to calculate the correct answer. The correct answer here, as with the first example, is choice (3).

All calculation questions like the one above are application questions, but not all application questions involve calculations. Also, while nearly all calculation questions will be straightforward multiple-choice questions, other application questions are just as likely to take the form of one of the other question types discussed in "An Overview of Question Types." For example, the following non-calculation application question takes the form of a two-statement combination question:

> Michelle Turner expects to receive $2,000 in a lump sum payment exactly four years from today. At 8 percent annual interest, the present value of that sum of money equals $1,470. The present value of that $2,000, however, can be affected by changes in the interest rate paid on it, and by changes in the amount of time that must pass before the money is received. It is correct to say that, with all other

factors that affect present value unchanged, the present value of the $2,000 will *increase* if

A. The interest rate paid on the $2,000 increases

B. The amount of time that must pass before Ms. Turner receives the $2,000 decreases

(1) Both A and B
(2) A only
(3) B only
(4) Neither A nor B

This application question asks you to think through, or predict, what would happen if the variables that determine the present value of a sum of money were altered. It obviously requires deeper thinking than a recognition type of question. The correct answer here is choice (3). This is because statement *A* is incorrect and statement *B* is correct, thereby making the correct answer choice "B only."

Statement *A* is incorrect because a higher interest rate will allow a smaller beginning sum of money (present value) to accumulate to a total of $2,000 in four years' time; for example, the present value of $2,000 to be received four years from today using a 15 percent annual interest rate equals $1,144. Statement *B* is correct, because with less time to accumulate to the desired level of $2,000, the beginning sum of money (present value) must be greater; for example, the present value of the $2,000 using an 8 percent interest rate and a one-year period equals $1,852.

Of course, not all application questions will be as complicated as the preceding question. Consider the following application question:

> William Scott named his children, Trudy and Bob, as primary beneficiaries to share equally in the proceeds of an insurance policy on his life. He also named his wife, Marlene, as the policy's contingent beneficiary. When William died, Trudy and Marlene were the only surviving beneficiaries. In this situation, the death benefit will be paid

(1) entirely to Trudy
(2) entirely to Marlene
(3) to Trudy and Marlene in equal shares
(4) to Trudy and to Bob's estate in equal shares

This question again asks you to predict an outcome based on a given set of facts. The correct answer here is choice (1), since all designated primary beneficiaries must predecease the contingent beneficiary before the contingent beneficiary is entitled to receive any benefits.

Consider one final calculation question:

> The offset approach is one method by which private pension plans can be integrated with government-sponsored pension plans. For example, Benjamin Quigley, a United States citizen, was enrolled in a private pension plan that promised to provide him with an income of $500 per month and that included a 50 percent Social Security offset. When Mr. Quigley retired, he was eligible to receive $400 per month from Social Security. In this situation, the private pension plan would pay Mr. Quigley a monthly benefit of

(1) $200
(2) $250
(3) $300
(4) $450

The correct answer here is choice (3), because 50 percent of Mr. Quigley's Social Security benefit (one-half of $400, or $200) would be subtracted from the $500 benefit promised by the private pension plan. This example also indicates that the incorrect answer choices in a calculation question are designed to catch those students who have not read the material. In other words, the incorrect answer choices are not pulled out of thin air by the examination specialist; they are usually based on the errors that the specialist thinks will be made by students who have not read the textual materials. For example, in this question, answer choice (1) equals 50 percent of the Social Security benefit, answer choice (2) equals 50 percent of the private plan's promised benefit, and answer choice (4) was calculated by reducing the $500 private benefit by 50 percent of the difference between the private plan's benefit and the Social Security benefit. All of these incorrect answer choices are designed to appear attractive as a "50 percent offset" to students who have not studied.

The preceding examples indicate that application questions are generally more difficult than recognition or definition questions. Therefore, it is important for you to realize that merely memorizing the definitions of concepts and key terms may no longer provide you with a deep enough understanding of the textual material to allow you to pass the FLMI examinations you take. You need to develop an understanding of how to apply the material to different situations. This undoubtedly will require more study on your part, but at the same time, a greater and deeper understanding of the concepts and principles involved in the life insurance industry will better prepare you for applying those principles in your everyday work environment. That is the main reason for the increased emphasis on application questions in FLMI examinations.

A NOTE ON MODIFICATION OF EXAMINATION FORMAT

All FLMI paper examinations except Course 9 contain 75 questions. Course 9 will continue to contain 57 questions. However, FLMI examinations will still rely on a 100-point scoring system. Under the 75-question format, each question is worth 1.333 points.

The reduction in the number of questions, without a corresponding reduction in the material to be covered by an examination, will lead examination specialists to focus even more efforts on developing application-oriented questions and on developing questions that integrate material from different parts of the assigned texts.

Although most I*STAR examinations may contain 75 questions, some I*STAR examinations may contain 100 questions. All I*STAR examinations have an applications emphasis.

AFTER THE EXAMINATION

Paper Examinations

If you have kept a record of your responses while you were in the examination room, you can further reinforce the knowledge that you have gained by looking up the correct answers in the textbook after you have completed the test and left the room. Of course, you will not be permitted to take your copy of the test with you when you leave the examination room. However, the proctor is authorized to return your copy of the test booklet to you after 24 hours have elapsed. Be sure that you put your name on the front of your test booklet so that you receive the same copy in which you kept a record of your responses.

While you are looking up the correct answers and more or less grading your performance, keep an eye out for any test items that you believe are incorrectly worded or for which the answer may not be entirely correct or clear. Here's why:

After your answer sheet has been returned to LOMA, the professionals who are responsible for developing the answer keys for the examinations receive letters from educational representatives who wish to challenge the validity of certain questions. The basis for such challenges varies — it may be a perception that a question is not clearly worded, or that the correct answer does not accurately reflect the textual passage on which it is based, or that the textual passage is at variance with current practices in the insurance industry. Infrequently, a typographical error may be cited as the basis for a challenge.

The important point to keep in mind about such challenges is that each one is investigated by the professional staff in the Education Division. If the staff committee doing the investigation finds that there is merit to the challenge — and the benefit of the doubt is always given to the student — that committee will recommend that the answer key be changed to give credit for more than one answer choice. The effect of such a recommendation is to give the students who chose the allowable responses credit for the challenged questions, regardless of whether the intended correct answer was chosen.

If you believe that there is good reason to challenge a test question after you have taken the test, put your challenge in writing and forward it to your educational representative, who will forward it to the Education Division for consideration. Be sure to submit any challenges so that they are received by the date specified in the Education Catalog and any resulting changes can be taken into account before answer sheets are scored. Once final grades are posted after that date, it is not possible to make any changes in them. You will be notified of the results of the investigation.

A few weeks after you have taken the test, you will receive a grade report through your educational representative. Your final grade may or may not correspond exactly with your own self-scored grade. If your final grade does not correspond, there may be several reasons why it does not. One such reason is that a challenge to an item from someone other than yourself may have been upheld, and you unknowingly benefited. Another, of course, is that your own list of answers, which you followed in self-scoring your own test, may have contained an error.

A third reason is that in the interest of ensuring fairness to the student, the Education Division creates various statistical reports designed to call to the staff's attention any irregularities in response patterns to questions. Each such irregularity is investigated in detail, to ensure that the reason for it is not some erroneous component of the question. If such an irregularity does lead to discovery of an error in a question, students will receive multiple credit for it. Of course, you would not be aware of key changes brought about by challenges from someone other than yourself or by similar changes brought about through investigations of statistical irregularities.

I*STAR Examinations

Administrative regulations pertaining to I*STAR examinations do not permit students to keep a record of their answer responses nor to transport any materials out of the testing room. Educational representatives or their designated proctors are required to collect all notes, scratch paper, etc., from students. These regulations are intended to enhance the security of an examination series available throughout the year.

I*STAR students, however, may still avail themselves of the opportunity to challenge test items. A student who believes that a test question is erroneous should record the question number and convey the challenge immediately to the educational representative, who will forward it to LOMA.

I*STAR examination results are subject to the same extensive statistical checks as are paper examination results.

Practice Questions

Practice makes perfect, so the adage goes, and nowhere is the adage truer than in the case of test preparation. This section is presented in order to give you the opportunity to practice answering questions of the types that you are likely to encounter in the actual examination.

The mode of presentation of the practice questions is uniform. For each chapter, there will be a series of test questions designed to provide fairly broad coverage of the central concepts presented in the law textbooks. Each chapter's practice questions and microcases may be based entirely on material from the chapter at hand, or they may also integrate material from other chapters or textbooks. Following the presentation of the questions for each chapter is a self-scoring key, which also lists the page(s) on which the correct answer to each of the questions can be found. Finally, there is a self-rating scale, designed to help you in rating your knowledge of the chapter.

Although the mode of presentation of the practice questions is uniform for each chapter, the number of questions is not. Some chapters are so short or so concentrated in coverage that only five or six questions are sufficient to test your knowledge of the concepts. In other cases, the chapters are so long or else so exhaustive in detail that as many as twelve to sixteen questions are required to provide adequate coverage.

You should not assume that the number of practice questions for a given chapter is indicative of the chapter's relative weight on the examination itself. Moreover, you should not assume that the fact that no practice question addresses a specific concept or fact presented in the chapter is an indication that the fact or concept is unimportant, or that it will not be the subject of a question on the test itself. Remember, a test is merely a sampling of knowledge. No test can hope to cover every fact or concept presented in the text(s) on which it is based. So, too, are these practice questions merely a sampling of knowledge. These questions are designed to provide an approximate measure of the breadth or depth of your knowledge of the chapters on which they are based. The questions make no pretense of providing thorough coverage of the chapters, although they do cover the breadth in terms of the text pages required to address the subject matter.

After you have read the text completely and are in the review process for each chapter, attempt to answer the practice questions on the chapter. Do not look at the scoring key for the questions until you have answered all the practice questions. Once you have answered the questions, turn to the scoring key and grade your question responses. Then check the self-rating scale to see where you stand in terms of your mastery of the chapter's contents.

Above all, do not stop there. For each question that you answered incorrectly, look up the correct answer. Determine why the response you chose is incorrect. In this way, you will be providing important reinforcement of the subject knowledge that you have gained. After all, it is the questions that we answer incorrectly on a test that we are likely to remember most after the test is over. The same principle works for these practice questions. Finally, if you chose an incorrect response because of an error of methodology in reading the question, go back to the introduction of this publication and review the section on methodology.

Once you have worked through all the practice questions in this section, determine for which chapters your performance was excellent or good. If your knowledge of any chapter was only fair or marginal or unsatisfactory, you should make a special effort to review the chapter in detail again before taking the 75-question practice test that appears at the end of this publication.

A final note: It is better to review the text and answer the practice questions one chapter at a time. Attempting to answer all the practice questions in one sitting, without the aid of a chapter-by-chapter review, defeats the purpose of the test preparation guide.

PRACTICE QUESTIONS
Chapter 1

1. Changes in populations and in family structures affect the marketing plans of life and health insurance companies. Current demographic trends in the United States and in Canada include

    (1) an increase in the average age of the population
    (2) a decrease in the number of working women
    (3) a decrease in the divorce rate
    (4) an increase in the death rate of people between the ages of 50 and 70 years old

2. The United States federal government did not become responsible for regulating the insurance industry until after the Supreme Court ruling in the case of *United States v. South-Eastern Underwriters Association* (1944). Before that ruling, the legal position of the federal government with respect to insurance regulation was that

    (1) insurance business was not considered to be a transaction in commerce
    (2) Congress prohibited the federal government from regulating commerce among the states
    (3) insurers were prohibited from conducting insurance business across state lines
    (4) Congress had declared that the regulation of insurance by the states was in the public interest

3. Organizations can influence insurance regulation without possessing the power of regulatory authority. In the United States, one such organization is the

    (1) Securities and Exchange Commission (SEC)
    (2) National Association of Insurance Commissioners (NAIC)
    (3) Office of the Superintendent of Financial Institutions (OSFI)
    (4) Association of Superintendents of Insurance (ASI)

4. In order for life and health insurance companies to become federally incorporated in Canada, these companies are required to

    (1) deposit reserve funds with the Canadian Council of Insurance Regulators
    (2) license their soliciting agents through the federal government
    (3) obtain a certificate of registry from the Minister of Finance
    (4) submit to an annual examination by the Office of the Superintendent of Financial Institutions to verify compliance with federal insurance statutes

5. Health maintenance organizations (HMOs) were developed in response to rising health care costs. An important concept behind the development of HMOs is that the HMO

    (1) accepts for membership only individuals who are also insured under a traditional health insurance plan which will share the risk with the HMO
    (2) gives its members an incentive to stay healthy, because it requires them to pay a high fixed percentage of all costs they incur under the plan
    (3) sets a low dollar-amount limit, usually between $500 and $1,500, on expenses it will pay in any one year on behalf of any plan member
    (4) has an incentive to hold down costs by keeping its members healthy, because its income is fixed, regardless of its level of expenses

6. In the United States, the National Association of Insurance Commissioners (NAIC) developed a zone system of examining insurance companies in order to

    (1) ensure that each state insurance department makes an annual independent examination of every insurance company operating in that state
    (2) examine insurance companies that operate in more than one state
    (3) ensure that insurance companies comply with the McCarran-Ferguson Act
    (4) regulate the marketing of investment-based insurance products

7. The following statement(s) can correctly be made about federal and provincial regulation of insurance in Canada:

    A. The provincial governments have the primary responsibility for ensuring the financial stability of both federally registered and provincially registered insurers
    B. The provincial insurance departments supervise the marketing of equity-based insurance products

    (1) Both A and B
    (2) A only
    (3) B only
    (4) Neither A nor B

8. In the United States, state insurance departments hold the primary legal authority over insurance company operations. State insurance departments are responsible for

    A. Making annual on-site examinations of each insurance company that operates within the state
    B. Maintaining an office for receiving and acting on consumer complaints
    C. Reviewing the Annual Statements of insurance companies
    D. Licensing agents to sell insurance products

    (1) All of these
    (2) A, B and C only
    (3) B, C and D only
    (4) A and D only
    (5) C and D only

ANSWERS TO PRACTICE QUESTIONS

Chapter 1

(1) 1, pp. 19-21
(2) 1, p. 13
(3) 2, p. 14
(4) 3, p. 17

(5) 4, p. 28
(6) 2, p. 14
(7) 3, p. 18
(8) 3, pp. 13-14, 16

SELF-RATING SCALE

If the number of correct answers is	Your knowledge of the chapter is
8	Excellent
7	Good
6	Marginal
5 or below	Unsatisfactory

PRACTICE QUESTIONS
Chapter 2

1. The Metronome Life and Health Insurance Company has a business relationship with a third-party administrator, the Adagio Group, in which Adagio provides administrative services to Metronome's group health insurance plans. This arrangement offers Metronome a cost-efficient way to gain Adagio's expertise in group plan administration. Both Metronome and Adagio retain their independence while sharing the risks and rewards of the relationship. Thus, the type of business relationship that Metronome has formed with Adagio is known as a

    (1) merger
    (2) strategic alliance
    (3) leveraged buyout
    (4) fraternal benefit society

2. The stock form of organization can offer a life and health insurance company several strategic advantages. However, one advantage that an insurance company **CANNOT** obtain from being organized as a stock company is the option to

    (1) increase its capital through the sale of additional shares of stock
    (2) offer shares of company stock as part of its executive compensation package
    (3) prevent another company from purchasing it in a takeover action
    (4) buy companies other than insurance companies without necessarily restricting those acquired companies to regulations meant only for insurers

3. Chuck Harrelson holds 25 shares of common stock and 40 shares of preferred stock in the Melisma Life Insurance Company. In its upcoming annual stockholders' meeting, Melisma is holding an election for its board of directors. Select the response that correctly identifies in the columns below whether Mr. Harrelson has voting rights in this election by virtue of his position as a common stockholder and as a preferred stockholder.

	Voting Rights as a Common Stockholder	Voting Rights as a Preferred Stockholder
(1)	yes	yes
(2)	yes	no
(3)	no	no
(4)	no	yes

4. The following statements are about the corporate form of business organization. Only one of these statements is false.

    A. All commercial insurance companies in the United States and in Canada are corporations
    B. A corporation continues beyond the death of any or all of its owners
    C. Corporations are considered to be distinct legal entities
    D. The owners of a corporation are personally liable for the debts of the corporation

    Of statements A, B, C, and D, the **FALSE** statement is

    (1) A
    (2) B
    (3) C
    (4) D

5. Ordinarily, holding companies may be formed either upstream or downstream from the company that forms them. Mutual life and health insurers that want to form holding companies

    (1) must first demutualize before they can form any holding company
    (2) can form only an upstream holding company
    (3) can form only a downstream holding company
    (4) can form either an upstream or a downstream holding company

6. The Prosit Life Assurance Company is seeking to incorporate in Canada, but it plans to do business only in the provinces of Manitoba and British Columbia. Prosit's home office will be located in the province of British Columbia. Once the company is licensed, one action that Prosit could take which would give Prosit the right to transact business in *both* provinces would be for Prosit to

    (1) file a memorandum of association with the federal government
    (2) apply to the federal department of insurance for all agents' licenses
    (3) file a memorandum of association with the government of British Columbia
    (4) seek federal incorporation under the Canada Business Corporations Act

7. The merger of two life and health insurance companies is said to produce *economies of scale* if the two companies

    (1) achieve a decrease in their unit costs as a result of combining their operations
    (2) incur enormous legal and accounting costs during the merger process
    (3) maintain their headquarters in separate locations
    (4) merge with the approval of at least two-thirds of their respective owners

8. The Rosehill Corporation is domiciled in Texas and it also conducts business in the states of Louisiana and Arkansas. From the viewpoint of the state of Louisiana, the Rosehill Corporation is considered to be

    (1) a foreign corporation
    (2) an alien corporation
    (3) a domestic corporation
    (4) a federal corporation

9. For a life and health insurance company, the process of mutualization involves

    (1) changing from a mutual company to a stock company
    (2) changing from a stock company to a mutual company
    (3) paying dividends to the owners of participating insurance policies
    (4) increasing its capital through the sale of additional shares of stock

10. In the United States and in Canada, fraternal benefit societies are legally required to use open insurance contracts. The term *open insurance contract* indicates that

    (1) amendments to the contract can diminish benefits that the society is contractually obligated to pay
    (2) the terms of the contract constitute the entire agreement between the policyowner and the society
    (3) the society's charter, constitution, and bylaws become a part of the contract
    (4) the society is exempt from the investment laws to which commercial insurers are subject

ANSWERS TO PRACTICE QUESTIONS

Chapter 2

(1) 2, p. 54
(2) 3, pp. 34-35, 40
(3) 2, p. 32
(4) 4, p. 36
(5) 3, p. 53

(6) 4, p. 38
(7) 1, p. 46
(8) 1, p. 37
(9) 2, p. 34
(10) 3, p. 59

SELF-RATING SCALE

If the number of correct answers is	Your knowledge of the chapter is
10	Excellent
9	Good
8	Fair
7	Marginal
6 or below	Unsatisfactory

PRACTICE QUESTIONS
Chapter 3

1. Takashi Yamada manages the human resources department at the Holbrook Life Insurance Company. Mr. Yamada has direct authority over John Worrell, an assistant in the human resources department. Mr. Yamada also has the authority to reject or to approve any requests for hiring new staff which are submitted by Jaclyn Zangretti, the manager of the claim administration department. Select the response below that correctly identifies for each column whether Mr. Yamada's authority over Mr. Worrell and over Ms. Zangretti is line authority or staff authority.

	Mr. Worrell	Ms. Zangretti
(1)	line	line
(2)	line	staff
(3)	staff	line
(4)	staff	staff

2. Diamond-shaped organizational structures have resulted from certain developments within life and health insurance companies. One such development is that, within a diamond-shaped organizational structure,

    (1) only the administrative support staff has access to word processing technology
    (2) large staffs of entry-level workers perform work functions that previously were performed by knowledge workers
    (3) fewer administrative support staff are needed because employees higher up in the organizational structure can perform certain administrative work functions themselves
    (4) sales agents must contact employees at the home office for policy information because sales agents are prevented from accessing such information electronically

3. As the manager of a word processing department, Martin Kincaid must ensure that the department fills all work requests within three days. Heavy workloads sometimes require hiring new employees or assigning overtime to current employees. However, Mr. Kincaid must obtain the approval of the human resources department in order to take either of these actions. Thus, Mr. Kincaid is unable to manage his department as effectively as possible. This information indicates that, in order to perform his job effectively, Mr. Kincaid would need greater

    (1) responsibility
    (2) authority
    (3) unity of command
    (4) accountability

4. The organizational structures of most life and health insurance companies can be characterized as either centralized or decentralized. One difference between a centralized and a decentralized organizational structure is that, within a *decentralized* organizational structure,

    (1) lower-level subordinates are granted less authority to make decisions
    (2) policies and actions throughout the organization tend to be more consistent because a single authority makes most decisions
    (3) managers can respond to situations quickly because they have a higher degree of authority to make decisions
    (4) certain administrative costs are reduced because a single department usually provides all administrative services

5. In a matrix organizational structure, personnel from product areas and from functional areas combine to work on a project. One characteristic of a matrix structure is that this organizational structure tends to

   (1) enhance commitment to a project from those employees who are involved in the project
   (2) inhibit the exchange of information
   (3) minimize overlap in the chain of authority and responsibility
   (4) ensure that employees are accountable to only one person

6. Within the Kirkwood Mutual Life Insurance Company, the legal department provides legal advice to all departments that produce Kirkwood's insurance products. Kirkwood's legal department does not provide legal advice to outside organizations. This information indicates that, in management terminology, Kirkwood's legal department can be classified as a

   (1) strategic business unit
   (2) staff unit
   (3) line unit
   (4) profit center

7. The Garland Health Insurance Company divides its operations into two separate business divisions — Group Health Insurance and Individual Health Insurance. Each of these divisions handles its own marketing, customer service, and underwriting activities. Centrally administered departments handle such functions as investments and accounting. This information indicates that, with respect to organizational structure, Garland is organized by

   (1) function, and this organizational structure tends to centralize Garland's operations
   (2) function, and this organizational structure tends to decentralize Garland's operations
   (3) product, and this organizational structure tends to centralize Garland's operations
   (4) product, and this organizational structure tends to decentralize Garland's operations

8. The boards of directors of life and health insurance companies often form standing committees. One such committee of the board supervises an insurance company's accounting operations and reviews the company's periodic financial statements. This committee is known as the

   (1) audit committee
   (2) tax committee
   (3) investment committee
   (4) executive committee

9. Many insurers are reorganizing their organizational structures to create flatter, rather than taller, organizational structures. One advantage of a flat organizational pyramid over a tall pyramid is that, in a *flat* organization,

   (1) employees have more opportunities for promotion
   (2) managers have closer control over the work of direct subordinates
   (3) employees lower down in the pyramid have more opportunities to make decisions that affect their own jobs
   (4) individual managers can be paid less because of decreased managerial responsibilities

10. A variety of factors determine whether a manager's span of control in a given situation should be broad or narrow. In general, one true statement about the breadth of a manager's span of control is that the

    (1) greater the physical distance of the subordinates from the manager, the greater the manager's span of control can be
    (2) higher the rate of turnover among subordinates, the greater the manager's span of control can be
    (3) less highly skilled and less competent subordinates are, the greater the manager's span of control can be
    (4) simpler and more repetitive subordinates' tasks are, the greater the manager's span of control can be

ANSWERS TO PRACTICE QUESTIONS

Chapter 3

(1) 2, pp. 76-77
(2) 3, p. 75
(3) 2, p. 64
(4) 3, p. 77
(5) 1, p. 85

(6) 2, p. 76
(7) 4, p. 78
(8) 1, p. 86
(9) 3, p. 72
(10) 4, p. 71

SELF-RATING SCALE

If the number of correct answers is	Your knowledge of the chapter is
10	Excellent
9	Good
8	Fair
7	Marginal
6 or below	Unsatisfactory

PRACTICE QUESTIONS
Chapter 4

1. The Yarborough Life Insurance Company focuses first on its consumers' needs and second on its products. Yarborough's marketing department studies the needs of the marketplace and then it develops and distributes the products that consumers want. Yarborough's marketing philosophy characterizes Yarborough as a

    (1) market-driven organization
    (2) sales-driven organization
    (3) price-driven organization
    (4) product-driven organization

2. If a life and health insurance company follows a differentiated target marketing strategy, then that company will

    (1) offer a variety of insurance products that are designed to appeal to different segments of the total market
    (2) produce only one insurance product and define the total market for that product as its target market
    (3) produce and distribute insurance products without evaluating the needs of the marketplace
    (4) focus all of its marketing resources on satisfying the needs of one segment of the total market for a particular type of insurance product

3. Marilyn Wall wants her family to receive a lump sum of $25,000 immediately after her death, a monthly income of $2,000 beginning upon her death and continuing until her youngest child is 21 years old, and, should she die before her husband, a monthly income of $1,200 thereafter for the remainder of her husband's life. Ms. Wall's insurance agent, Earl Robert, is determining how much new insurance, with allowances for her current insurance coverage and for anticipated government-provided benefits, that Ms. Wall will require to meet these needs. This information indicates that Mr. Robert is engaged in the mode of selling known as

    (1) single-need selling
    (2) readjustment funding
    (3) concentrated marketing
    (4) total-needs programming

4. When developing a marketing plan, an insurer must consider several factors in its external environment. One aspect of the external environment includes such factors as a nation's inflation rate, prevailing and forecasted interest rates, and unemployment levels. These factors are part of an insurer's

    (1) regulatory environment
    (2) economic environment
    (3) technological environment
    (4) societal environment

5. The Gemstone Life Insurance Company segmented the market for an insurance product in terms of consumers' age and their preferred method of purchase. Gemstone's defined market for this product includes individuals who are over age 50 and who prefer to purchase insurance products through direct response marketing. This information indicates that the two bases for market segmentation that Gemstone used in this instance are

   (1) geographic segmentation and psychographic segmentation
   (2) lifestyle segmentation and demographic segmentation
   (3) demographic segmentation and behavioristic segmentation
   (4) psychographic segmentation and geographic segmentation

6. Four internal factors that affect a life and health insurance company's marketing plan are the company's existing products, its current distribution systems, its corporate culture, and its financial condition. Of these internal factors, the factor that typically changes most on a year-to-year basis is the company's

   (1) existing products
   (2) current distribution systems
   (3) corporate culture
   (4) financial condition

7. Perry Russo, a life insurance agent, induced Sara Navdeep to discontinue her life insurance policy and to use the cash value to purchase a new policy. Mr. Russo misled Ms. Navdeep by not clearly informing her of the differences between the two policies and of the negative financial consequences of replacing the original policy. In this situation, Mr. Russo engaged in the prohibited sales practice known as

   (1) replacement
   (2) rebating
   (3) twisting
   (4) guaranteeing policy dividends

ANSWERS TO PRACTICE QUESTIONS

Chapter 4

(1) 1, p. 96
(2) 1, p. 110
(3) 4, p. 118
(4) 2, p. 104
(5) 3, pp. 109-110
(6) 4, p. 104
(7) 3, p. 122

SELF-RATING SCALE

If the number of correct answers is	Your knowledge of the chapter is
7	Excellent
6	Good
5	Marginal
4 or below	Unsatisfactory

PRACTICE QUESTIONS
Chapter 5

1. Although service fees are a form of renewal compensation to insurance agents, they differ from renewal commissions in some respects. Typically, one difference is that *service fees* are

    (1) paid to the agent who is currently providing service to the policyowner, regardless of who sold the policy, whereas renewal commissions are paid to the agent who sold the policy
    (2) vested to the agent who sold the policy, whereas renewal commissions are rarely vested
    (3) paid to home service agents only, whereas renewal commissions are paid to any soliciting agent who has sold a policy
    (4) paid to the agent who is currently providing service to the policyowner, but only if that agent sold the policy, whereas renewal commissions are paid to the servicing agent, regardless of who sold the policy

2. Although branch managers and general agents both manage field offices for life insurance companies, their functions differ in some respects. One difference between the branch manager and the general agent is that only the *branch manager* usually is

    (1) actively involved in personal life insurance sales
    (2) compensated partly in the form of a monthly salary from the life insurance company
    (3) an independent contractor who is under contract to the life insurance company
    (4) responsible for providing the funds to pay for all office expenses and salaries

3. In developing an operating plan for his life insurance agency, Emilio Sanchez prepared a report wherein he presented the following estimates:

    * the number of sales agents that his agency would require to produce a projected sales level
    * the sales agents' future salaries and commissions
    * the time and money needed to train three new sales agents

    In this situation, Mr. Sanchez developed the part of an agency's operating plan that is known as

    (1) an operating budget
    (2) a functional cost analysis
    (3) a staffing schedule
    (4) a career profile system

4. In order to gain more control over soliciting agents' compensation within the general agency system, many insurers have revised their method of paying overriding commissions. In current general agency contracts, many insurers now pay commissions directly to

    (1) soliciting agents and overriding commissions directly to general agents
    (2) general agents, who are responsible for paying commissions to soliciting agents
    (3) soliciting agents, who are responsible for paying overriding commissions to general agents
    (4) soliciting agents, and general agents no longer receive overriding commissions

5. Studies have shown that, in general, people who are successful as insurance agents possess certain characteristics. For instance, successful insurance agents typically

    (1) are unmarried
    (2) possess college degrees
    (3) have no previous sales experience
    (4) enter the business between the ages of 20 and 25

6. Role playing is one instructional technique that life and health insurance companies use to train new sales agents. In role playing, a new agent

    (1) attends lectures about the fundamentals of insurance sales
    (2) takes a test that predicts the new agent's likelihood for success as an insurance agent
    (3) acts out a selling situation with a manager or a trainer who assumes the role of a prospect and leads the new agent to the solution of a sales problem
    (4) goes on sales calls with an agency manager or an experienced agent who provides the new agent with advice and moral support

7. A life insurance company might choose to distribute its products through a general agency system rather than through a branch office system. In a *general agency* system, the life insurance company typically

    (1) exercises greater control over its marketing plans than the insurer typically can exercise in a branch office system
    (2) can transfer field office personnel from one territory to another territory
    (3) can change the field office territory at any time
    (4) assumes less than the full costs associated with establishing new field offices, whereas the insurer typically must pay the full costs of establishing a new branch office

8. Within the multiple-line agency (MLA) system, sales agents are able to cross-sell a variety of insurance products. Cross-selling reflects a change in the insurance industry's approach to conducting business. Specifically, the MLA system reflects the industry's movement from

    (1) a product-centered orientation to a more customer-centered orientation
    (2) a market-driven orientation to a more product-driven orientation
    (3) an agency-building orientation to a more non-agency-building orientation
    (4) a customer-centered orientation to a more product-centered orientation

9. An agency manager for a life insurance company is responsible for developing the operating plan that guides the agency's operations. The operating budget, which is one part of the operating plan, contains estimates of the

    (1) time and money that is needed for recruiting, hiring, and training new agents
    (2) levels of new and renewal business that the agency expects to produce
    (3) number of agents and office personnel that are needed to produce a projected amount of business
    (4) average operating costs in other agencies of the same size

10. Although the ordinary agency system and the home service system are similar in many ways, they differ in certain areas. One typical difference is that, unlike agents in the ordinary agency system, agents in the *home service* system are

    (1) permitted to sell only industrial insurance policies
    (2) prohibited from collecting renewal premiums from policyowners
    (3) expected to spend a relatively small portion of their time on recordkeeping and on providing policyowner service
    (4) responsible for transferring the records of policyowners who move out of their territories

ANSWERS TO PRACTICE QUESTIONS

Chapter 5

(1) 1, p. 149
(2) 2, pp. 131, 150
(3) 3, p. 135
(4) 1, p. 133
(5) 2, p. 136

(6) 3, p. 138
(7) 4, pp. 133-34
(8) 1, p. 153
(9) 2, p. 135
(10) 4, p. 158

SELF-RATING SCALE

If the number of correct answers is	Your knowledge of the chapter is
10	Excellent
9	Good
8	Fair
7	Marginal
6 or below	Unsatisfactory

PRACTICE QUESTIONS
Chapter 6

1. The Metropolis Health Insurance Company is marketing a long-term care insurance policy to targeted individuals. Metropolis is mailing each prospect an introduction letter, a brochure with detailed product information, and an insurance application. Any prospect who returns a completed insurance application will not be denied insurance coverage for health-related reasons. This information indicates that Metropolis is promoting its insurance product through

    (1) telemarketing, and the product is offered on a noncontributory basis
    (2) telemarketing, and the product is offered on a guaranteed-issue basis
    (3) direct response marketing, and the product is offered on a noncontributory basis
    (4) direct response marketing, and the product is offered on a guaranteed-issue basis

2. The following statements are about the use of direct response advertising to distribute insurance products. Only one of these statements is true.

    A. People who have already purchased goods or services through direct response advertising are likely to continue making such purchases
    B. Direct response advertising seeks only to build an awareness and a positive image of an insurance company, rather than to elicit an immediate reaction from consumers
    C. Direct response insurance companies seldom target senior citizens because they present a high health risk
    D. Underwriting requirements for direct response insurance products are typically complex

    Of statements A, B, C, and D, the **TRUE** statement is

    (1) A
    (2) B
    (3) C
    (4) D

3. The nature of group insurance and the characteristics of its market necessitate a marketing approach that differs from the marketing of individual insurance products. One difference between the marketing of group insurance products and the marketing of individual insurance products is that, in the marketing of *group* insurance products, the

    (1) prospect is less likely to be informed about insurance products than is a prospect for individual insurance products
    (2) sales agent is more likely to be a salaried employee of the insurance company than is a sales agent for individual insurance products
    (3) insurance contracts are more standardized than are individual insurance contracts
    (4) insurance contracts provide a smaller total amount of coverage than do individual insurance contracts

4. As an agent-broker, Malcolm Levin sells the life insurance products of more than one life insurance company. If Mr. Levin's relationship with these life insurance companies is typical of the brokerage distribution system, then he

    (1) is compensated partly in the form of service fees
    (2) works out of a life insurance company's branch office
    (3) is compensated primarily on a commissioned basis
    (4) receives career training and office support from the life insurance companies

5. The Parkland Corporation has a noncontributory group life insurance plan for its employees. The fact that the plan is noncontributory indicates both who will pay the insurance premiums and who will enroll in the plan. Because Parkland's group plan is noncontributory, enrollment of eligible group members must be

   (1) automatic, and Parkland must pay the entire insurance premium
   (2) automatic, and the group members must pay a portion of the insurance premium
   (3) voluntary, and Parkland must pay the entire insurance premium
   (4) voluntary, and the group members must pay a portion of the insurance premium

6. Concerning group life and health insurance, the term that is used to describe all of the activities from the time a prospect decides to purchase a group insurance policy to the time the master group policy and its individual certificates are issued and delivered is

   (1) prospecting
   (2) installation
   (3) conservation
   (4) enrollment

7. Insurers use salaried sales personnel to distribute certain types of products, including

   A. Fraternal life insurance products
   B. Pension products
   C. Group life insurance products
   D. Savings bank life insurance products

   (1) All of these
   (2) A, B and D only
   (3) A, C and D only
   (4) B and C only
   (5) C only

8. One difference between print media advertising and direct mail advertising is that *print media* advertising typically enables marketers to

   (1) target a more specifically defined market
   (2) achieve higher response rates
   (3) achieve a lower cost per person exposed to the advertising
   (4) code advertisements and trace each response to its source advertisement, whereas direct mail advertisements cannot be coded

9. The location selling distribution system for marketing insurance products relies on

   (1) brokerage shops to solicit substandard business from agent-brokers
   (2) independent agents to initiate contact with prospects through in-home sales presentations
   (3) consumers to initiate insurance purchases by calling toll-free telephone numbers and requesting information about insurance products
   (4) consumers to initiate insurance purchases by visiting insurance offices that are placed where consumers shop for other items

10. In some respects, insurers that use the personal-producing general agent (PPGA) distribution system operate similarly to insurers that use the brokerage distribution system. However, some differences exist between the two systems. Unlike insurers that use the brokerage distribution system, insurers that exclusively use the *PPGA* system

    (1) are classified as agency-building companies
    (2) are responsible for managing and controlling the operations of agencies
    (3) rarely establish minimum production requirements for their agents
    (4) offer their agents contracts that more closely resemble a general agent's contract than a soliciting agent's contract

11. Although Eugenie Blouin is a full-time agent for the Parish Life Insurance Company, Ms. Blouin on occasion submits an insurance application to life insurance companies other than Parish. Because Parish declined one life insurance application, Ms. Blouin placed the business through an independent agency that specializes in substandard business through a variety of life insurance companies. In this situation, by placing business through this agency with an insurer other than Parish, Ms. Blouin is engaging in the activity of

   (1) prospecting, and she is placing business through a brokerage manager
   (2) conservation, and she is placing business through a group representative
   (3) brokering business, and she is placing business through a brokerage shop
   (4) debiting, and she is placing business through an advanced underwriting unit

ANSWERS TO PRACTICE QUESTIONS

Chapter 6

(1) 4, pp. 173, 175, 177
(2) 1, pp. 175-76
(3) 2, p. 169
(4) 3, p. 166
(5) 1, p. 171
(6) 2, p. 170

(7) 1, pp. 169, 172-73
(8) 3, pp. 177-78
(9) 4, pp. 162, 179
(10) 4, p. 168
(11) 3, pp. 164-65

SELF-RATING SCALE

If the number of correct answers is	Your knowledge of the chapter is
11	Excellent
10	Good
9	Fair
8	Marginal
7 or below	Unsatisfactory

PRACTICE QUESTIONS
Chapter 7

1. Predicted results are more likely to match actual results if a person examines four million occurrences than if that person examines only four occurrences. This fact illustrates the concept known as the

    (1) selection of risks
    (2) present value theory
    (3) law of large numbers
    (4) projection method

2. When performing asset share calculations on a new individual life insurance product, actuaries typically select a conservative mortality table and a conservative interest rate to calculate the product's reserves. Then, to calculate the product's premium, actuaries typically select a mortality table that is more

    (1) liberal and an interest rate that is lower than those selected to calculate the product's reserves
    (2) liberal and an interest rate that is higher than those selected to calculate the product's reserves
    (3) conservative and an interest rate that is lower than those selected to calculate the product's reserves
    (4) conservative and an interest rate that is higher than those selected to calculate the product's reserves

3. Life and health insurance companies typically categorize the various operating expenses that are allocated to insurance products. The category of *termination* expenses includes the costs of

    (1) processing applications for insurance and issuing insurance policies to policyowners
    (2) planning and creating insurance products
    (3) keeping insurance policies in force
    (4) processing death benefit claims and cash surrenders

4. To calculate mortality rates for annuity contracts, actuaries will incorporate a safety margin into a mortality table by

    (1) adjusting the mortality rates to show fewer people dying at each age than are actually expected to die
    (2) adjusting the mortality rates to show more people dying at each age than are actually expected to die
    (3) measuring the probabilities of dying, rather than the probabilities of living, for a large group of people
    (4) presenting the mortality experience of the general population, rather than the mortality experience of specific groups of people

5. In the Commissioners 1980 Standard Ordinary mortality table, the mortality rate for 50-year-old females is 4.96. This information indicates that, in a given year,

    (1) 4.96 out of 100,000 50-year-old women can be expected to die
    (2) 496 out of 1,000 50-year-old women can be expected to die
    (3) 496 out of 100,000 50-year-old women can be expected to die
    (4) 4,960 out of 100,000 50-year-old women can be expected to die

6. In the life insurance industry, mortality tables without safety margins are known as

   (1) table *a* mortality tables
   (2) Commissioners Standard Ordinary mortality tables
   (3) valuation mortality tables
   (4) basic mortality tables

7. The Charlemagne Life Insurance Group invested $200,000 at an annual simple interest rate of 10 percent. At the same time, Charlemagne invested $200,000 in an investment that earns an interest rate of 10 percent that is compounded annually. Charlemagne neither deposited nor withdrew any money from these investments. Select the response that correctly identifies in the columns below the total amount of interest that Charlemagne's investments will earn after two years of earning simple interest and compound interest, respectively.

	Simple Interest Earnings	Compound Interest Earnings
(1)	$4,000	$4,200
(2)	$20,000	$22,000
(3)	$40,000	$42,000
(4)	$42,000	$40,000

8. Most life and health insurance companies conduct studies of lapse rates among their policyowners. Such studies show that lapse rates tend to be lower among policyowners

   (1) with low incomes than with high incomes
   (2) in the younger age groups than among senior citizens
   (3) who make monthly premium payments pay through a preauthorized check system rather than on a mail-in basis
   (4) who make monthly premium payments rather than annual premium payments

* * * * * *

Questions 9 through 11 are matching questions. Life insurance companies require actuaries to perform a variety of calculations. In the left-hand column are descriptions of various calculations that actuaries must make with respect to individual life insurance products. Choose the term from the right-hand column that matches each description.

9. A statutory fund made up of assets and future premiums to be received from in-force life insurance policies in order to pay future claims on those policies

10. A charge added to the net premium of a life insurance policy in order to pay for the insurer's operating expenses

11. The amount of money that an insurer guarantees to pay to a life insurance policyowner if the policyowner cancels the insurance coverage and surrenders the policy to the insurer

(1) Cash value

(2) Surplus

(3) Loading

(4) Policy dividend

(5) Policy reserve

12. The process an actuary uses for calculating the amount of money that a life and health insurance company needs to invest today in order to accumulate a specific amount of money by a specified future date is known as

    (1) loading
    (2) selection of risks
    (3) discounting
    (4) rate making

13. When conducting asset share calculations on a new individual life insurance product, actuaries will forecast the product's validation point. Until a new life insurance product reaches its validation point, the product's

    (1) total revenue exceeds its total expenses
    (2) policy reserves exceed its asset share
    (3) net premiums equal its gross premiums
    (4) premium income exceeds the amount of money that is paid out in claims, cash surrenders, and expenses

ANSWERS TO PRACTICE QUESTIONS

Chapter 7

(1) 3, p. 187
(2) 2, p. 210
(3) 4, p. 200
(4) 1, p. 191
(5) 3, p. 188
(6) 4, p. 191
(7) 3, p. 196

(8) 3, p. 204
(9) 5, pp. 197, 206
(10) 3, pp. 199-200
(11) 1, pp. 206-07
(12) 3, p. 197
(13) 2, p. 211

SELF-RATING SCALE

If the number of correct answers is	Your knowledge of the chapter is
13	Excellent
12	Good
11	Fair
10	Marginal
9 or below	Unsatisfactory

PRACTICE QUESTIONS
Chapter 8

1. Whether a group is large or small affects the approach that an insurer will take in determining initial premium rates for group life insurance. If a group is small, insurers typically would determine the initial premium rate on the basis of

    (1) manual rates
    (2) blended rates
    (3) the group's prior claim experience
    (4) each group member's family health history

2. Actuaries are predicting the annual claim costs for a block of one-year hospital expense policies for 2,000 men who are 50 years old. The actuaries predict that 200 of these men will file a claim, and that the average claim will be for $1,000. This information indicates that the predicted annual claim cost for this block of policies is

    (1) $100
    (2) $200,000
    (3) $1,800,000
    (4) $2,000,000

3. The following statements can correctly be made about group life insurance policies:

    A. These policies typically build cash value
    B. Premiums for these policies are typically paid on a monthly basis
    C. The majority of these policies are issued as one-year renewable term insurance
    D. The individuals insured under these policies are actual parties to the master contract

            (1) A, C and D only
            (2) A, B and D only
            (3) A and C only
            (4) B and C only
            (5) B and D only

4. In the life and health insurance industry, the primary purpose of continuance tables is to provide actuaries with

    (1) manual rates that are based on the mortality experience of an average group
    (2) blended rates that are based partly on manually rated data and partly on experience-rated data
    (3) morbidity statistics that indicate the distribution of claims according to the duration of the illness or to the amount of expense involved in the claims
    (4) mortality statistics that indicate how policy reserves would accumulate under various experience scenarios

5. Several states specify the minimum initial gross premium that an insurer must charge a group that has never been covered by any group life insurance contract. In these states, the minimum premium rates apply only to group life insurance contracts that were issued on a

    (1) term basis and these rates apply only in the first policy year
    (2) whole life basis and these rates apply only in the first policy year
    (3) term basis and these rates apply for as long as the group remains covered by the initial insurance carrier
    (4) whole life basis and these rates apply for as long as the group remains covered by the initial insurance carrier

6. An actuary is calculating the premium rates for a group health insurance contract. The following information is available about the group:

   Claim frequency rate per insured .... 20 percent
   Average dollar amount per claim $300
   Number of insured lives 50

   The amount of aggregate claims expected from this group is

   (1) $370
   (2) $3,000
   (3) $15,000
   (4) $300,000

7. Special group insurance reserves are sometimes created for specific purposes. For example, a claim fluctuation reserve for a group insurance contract is established by an

   (1) insured group for the purpose of paying future premiums
   (2) insured group for the purpose of paying the administrative expenses of the insurance contract
   (3) insurer for the purpose of providing for possible unfavorable claim experience in the future years of the insurance contract
   (4) insurer for the purpose of providing for the administrative expenses of processing the group's claims

ANSWERS TO PRACTICE QUESTIONS

Chapter 8

(1) 1, p. 217
(2) 2, p. 224
(3) 4, pp. 215, 218
(4) 3, p. 195
(5) 1, p. 217
(6) 2, p. 222
(7) 3, pp. 220-21

SELF-RATING SCALE

If the number of correct answers is	Your knowledge of the chapter is
7	Excellent
6	Good
5	Marginal
4 or below	Unsatisfactory

PRACTICE QUESTIONS
Chapter 9

1. When one type of reinsurance treaty is made, the treaty specifies at the outset the respective percentages of the risk that will be carried by the ceding company and by the reinsurer. This type of reinsurance plan is

    (1) stop-loss reinsurance and it tends to be used in connection with individual insurance
    (2) proportional reinsurance and it tends to be used in connection with individual insurance
    (3) catastrophic reinsurance and it tends to be used in connection with group insurance
    (4) nonproportional reinsurance and it tends to be used in connection with group insurance

2. A group underwriter for life and health insurance is primarily concerned that a proposed group present a good distribution of risk. A group with a good distribution of risk is one in which

    (1) the good health of a large number of group members offsets the claim experience of the unhealthy group members
    (2) each group member provides evidence of insurability and each member is individually underwritten
    (3) substandard or uninsurable risks are ineligible for group insurance coverage
    (4) a higher-than-average percentage of participants are in poorer-than-average health

3. In life insurance underwriting, the risk class to which an insured is assigned indicates the level of premium rate that the insured pays. Four common risk classes in the life insurance industry are

    A. Substandard
    B. Preferred
    C. Standard

    Beginning with the risk class containing the insureds who pay the *lowest* premium rates and ending with the risk class containing the insureds who pay the highest premium rates, the correct order of these risk classes is

    (1) A—B—C
    (2) A—C—B
    (3) B—C—A
    (4) C—B—A

4. The Walden Life Insurance Company has set $500,000 as the maximum amount of life insurance that it will carry at its own risk on any one individual. Thus, $500,000 is Walden Life's

    (1) stop-loss limit
    (2) net amount at risk
    (3) retention limit
    (4) automatic binding limit

5. In the life and health insurance industry, the term *retrocessionaire* refers to

    (1) a reinsurance company that accepts the excess risk of another reinsurance company
    (2) an insurance company that accepts a risk from an assuming company
    (3) a reinsurance company that is seeking to reinsure its excess risk
    (4) an insurance company employee who is responsible for arranging and administering reinsurance agreements

6. The Elysian Life Insurance Company uses a typical numerical rating system to assign proposed life insureds to underwriting risk classes. Elysian uses a basic rating value of 100. Elysian assigned the following values on Ernestine Smoot's application for life insurance:

Factor	Rating	
	Debit	Credit
Basic Rating	100	
Build	30	
Girth	20	
Family History		30
Subtotal	150	30

This information indicates that Ms. Smoot will be assigned a total numerical rating of

(1) 80 points and she will be classified as a preferred risk
(2) 120 points and she will be classified as a standard risk
(3) 150 points and she will be classified as a substandard risk
(4) 180 points and she will be classified as an uninsurable risk

7. When evaluating a group's eligibility for group insurance, life and health insurance companies typically evaluate whether the group meets certain underwriting standards. One typical underwriting standard for group insurance is that a group must

(1) pay the entire premium for insurance coverage on its eligible members
(2) have been formed for the purpose of purchasing insurance
(3) expect a sufficient inflow of young new members to replace those members who leave the group
(4) allow its group members to choose the amount of their insurance protection

8. In underwriting for life and health insurance companies, a jet screening staff can approve certain insurance applications for immediate policy issue. However, if an insurance application does **NOT** meet the criteria for immediate issue, then the jet screening staff typically would

(1) decline or rate the application
(2) give the application to an underwriter for evaluation
(3) attach an impairment rider to the insurance policy
(4) return the application to the sales agent for additional information gathering

9. The following statements can correctly be made about medical risk factors for underwriting life insurance:

A. The majority of rated life insurance policies are rated for medical, rather than nonmedical, reasons
B. The likelihood of physical Impairment generally decreases as a person ages
C. A person who is underweight generally represents a greater mortality risk than does a person who is overweight
D. Cigarette smoking generally increases a person's mortality risk

(1) A, C and D only
(2) A and B only
(3) A and D only
(4) B and C only
(5) C and D only

10. The Atlee Life Insurance Company has a reinsurance arrangement with the Topaz Reinsurance Company. For each risk that it cedes to Topaz, Atlee pays Topaz part of the premium paid by the insured, minus an allowance for Atlee's expenses. In return, Topaz agrees to pay Atlee a proportionate part of the death benefit when a claim is filed. In addition, Topaz accumulates the required reserves for the reinsured portion of the policy. This information indicates that Atlee and Topaz are using the type of reinsurance plan that is known as a

    (1) stop-loss reinsurance plan
    (2) coinsurance plan
    (3) yearly renewable term plan
    (4) modified coinsurance plan

11. The following proposed life insureds were classified as substandard risks:

    * Marita Alonzo is overweight
    * Ed Benavides had tuberculosis one year previously but he shows no signs of current infection
    * Malone Candace suffers from the acquired immune deficiency syndrome (AIDS)
    * Lamar DeVinney has untreated high blood pressure and his condition is expected to worsen as he grows older

    Underwriters generally would use the flat extra premium method in order to determine life insurance premium rates for only

    (1) Ms. Alonzo
    (2) Mr. Benavides
    (3) Ms. Candace
    (4) Mr. DeVinney

12. The assignment of a proposed life insured to the preferred risk class indicates whether that individual presents an acceptable risk to the life insurer and, if so, the level of premium rates that will be applied to the coverage. Typically, a person who is assigned to the preferred risk class is

    (1) declined insurance coverage
    (2) accepted for insurance coverage at standard premium rates
    (3) accepted for insurance coverage at higher-than-standard premium rates
    (4) accepted for insurance coverage at lower-than-standard premium rates

13. The Angleton Life Insurance Company and the Zapata Life Insurance Company have entered into a reinsurance treaty. Under the terms of the treaty, Zapata can decide which policies it will accept from Angleton and which policies it will decline. Select the response that correctly identifies in the columns below the type of reinsurance treaty and whether Angleton is the ceding company or the reinsurer in this arrangement.

	Treaty Type	Angleton's Role
(1)	automatic	reinsurer
(2)	automatic	ceding company
(3)	facultative	reinsurer
(4)	facultative	ceding company

14. One source of information for a life or health insurance underwriter is an inspection report. An inspection report is prepared by

    (1) a physician and it contains specific information about a proposed insured's health history
    (2) a sales agent and it contains information about a proposed insured's occupation, personal habits, and hobbies
    (3) the Medical Information Bureau and it contains specific information about a proposed insured's health history
    (4) a consumer reporting agency and it contains information about a proposed insured's occupation, personal habits, and hobbies

15. In determining renewal premium rates for group life or health insurance policies, an underwriter typically takes into account a group's past claims. This process of considering a group's past claims to develop premium rates is known as

    (1) retrocession
    (2) manual rating
    (3) claim rating
    (4) experience rating

16. Insurers include pre-existing condition provisions in their individual health insurance policies in order to

    (1) protect themselves from the risk of antiselection
    (2) ensure that a policy remains in force for a specified minimum period, usually one or two years
    (3) provide benefits for health conditions that were initially treated before a policy's issue date
    (4) prevent insureds from purchasing more insurance than is necessary

ANSWERS TO PRACTICE QUESTIONS

Chapter 9

(1) 2, p. 264
(2) 1, p. 257
(3) 3, pp. 245-46
(4) 3, p. 261
(5) 1, p. 261
(6) 2, pp. 249-50
(7) 3, p. 258
(8) 2, p. 236

(9) 3, pp. 240, 242
(10) 2, p. 265
(11) 2, p. 252
(12) 4, p. 246
(13) 4, pp. 260, 263
(14) 4, p. 239
(15) 4, p. 259
(16) 1, p. 255

SELF-RATING SCALE

If the number of correct answers is	Your knowledge of the chapter is
16	Excellent
15	Good
14	Fair
13	Marginal
12 or below	Unsatisfactory

PRACTICE QUESTIONS
Chapter 10

1. In order to become insured under a group insurance plan, each group member must complete an enrollment card that provides the insurer with demographic information about the new member. If the group insurance plan is administered by the insurer, then the enrollment cards are maintained by

    (1) the group policyholder
    (2) a third-party administrator
    (3) the insurer's group representative
    (4) the insurer's customer service department

2. In the United States, insurers sometimes promote 1035 exchanges to policyowners who want to replace a life insurance policy with another insurer's policy. One benefit to a policyowner of a 1035 exchange is that the 1035 exchange

    (1) allows the policyowner to improve a current policy so that the alternative of replacement becomes unattractive
    (2) allows the policyowner to increase a current policy's death benefit without increasing the policy's premiums
    (3) insulates the policyowner from any tax effect in replacing one policy with another like policy
    (4) allows a policy's cash value to earn interest and dividends at a current yield without increasing the policy's premiums

3. Many individual life insurance policies give the policyowner the right to change coverage from one type of policy to another. For example, a policyowner may be allowed to change a term life insurance policy to a whole life insurance policy. The type of transaction that is used in order to change the policyowner's insurance coverage in this manner is termed a

    (1) reissue
    (2) policy update
    (3) reinstatement
    (4) policy conversion

4. Anna Dubac is the policyowner-insured of a participating life insurance policy. When Ms. Dubac applied for the policy in 1990, she elected to receive her policy dividends in cash. Ms. Dubac wants to change her dividend option and use the dividends to buy one-year term life insurance. Upon receiving Ms. Dubac's request, the life insurance company will most likely

    (1) require evidence of insurability from Ms. Dubac before approving or denying her request
    (2) immediately approve and process the request without restrictions
    (3) deny the request, because dividend options can be changed only during the first year that a policy is in force
    (4) deny the request, because dividend options cannot be changed during the life of a policy

5. A life and health insurance company's customers can be classified as external customers and internal customers. A life and health insurance company's *internal* customers include the company's

    (1) target markets
    (2) group policyholders
    (3) individual policyowners
    (4) customer service representatives

Questions 6 and 7 are matching questions. Customer service departments in life and health insurance companies can be structured in a variety of ways. In the left-hand column are names of various organizational structures. From the right-hand column, select the answer that describes each of these methods of structuring the customer service function.

6. Functional organization

7. Product organization

(1) Customer service personnel are trained in certain product lines and work with only those products

(2) Each agent and policyowner is assigned to a specific unit or to a specific staff member in the customer service department

(3) Each customer service specialist performs one task or a few tasks that are similar in nature

(4) The customer service department is divided into sections that serve only customers in specific regions

* * * * * *

8. A number of life and health insurance companies use the team structure for the customer service department. One characteristic of team organization is that, in this structure,

   (1) both the customer base and the team staff must be small
   (2) team members typically plan their own work and vacation schedules
   (3) all team decisions typically are made and implemented without any management involvement
   (4) managers are left with inadequate time for planning and dealing with unusual occurrences

9. Policyowners who have purchased their insurance coverage through direct response methods receive most of their information and assistance from the insurer's

   (1) brokers
   (2) field agents
   (3) group representatives
   (4) customer service department

ANSWERS TO PRACTICE QUESTIONS

Chapter 10

(1) 4, p. 297
(2) 3, p. 291
(3) 4, p. 284
(4) 1, pp. 289-90
(5) 4, p. 272

(6) 3, p. 277
(7) 1, p. 278
(8) 2, p. 282
(9) 4, p. 273

SELF-RATING SCALE

If the number of correct answers is	Your knowledge of the chapter is
9	Excellent
8	Good
7	Fair
6	Marginal
5 or below	Unsatisfactory

PRACTICE QUESTIONS
Chapter 11

1. In order to process a life insurance claim, life insurance companies require a completed claim form and proof of the insured's death. In certain situations, a life insurance company may also request an Attending Physician's Statement and an autopsy report. Life insurance companies typically would request these additional documents in a situation in which the

    (1) policy provides for accidental death benefits
    (2) insured had died after the contestable period expired
    (3) claimant had submitted a certified copy of the death certificate rather than the original death certificate
    (4) insured had died while the policy's premium payments were overdue

2. An insurer who seeks the legal remedy of rescission is asking the court to

    (1) approve the surveillance of a disability income claimant who is suspected of fraud
    (2) cancel an insurance contract on the ground that no valid contract ever existed
    (3) determine the proper recipient of a claim settlement
    (4) lengthen the time during which the insurer can challenge the validity of an insurance contract

3. Although fewer than one percent of all life insurance claims are denied, an insurer would probably deny such a claim if the insured had

    A. Committed suicide after the policy's suicide exclusion period expired
    B. Died during the policy's contestable period and information that was material to underwriting the policy had not been disclosed on the policy application

    (1) Both A and B
    (2) A only
    (3) B only
    (4) Neither A nor B

4. Howard Dean became disabled recently while insured under his employer's disability income insurance plan. If the plan uses the definition of total disability used in most disability income policies that are issued today, then Mr. Dean will be considered totally disabled

    (1) only if his disability prevents him from working in any occupation, and then only if his disability is determined to be permanent
    (2) for as long as his disability prevents him from working full-time or from completing certain important job duties
    (3) for an initial specified period, only if his disability prevents him from working at any occupation for which he is reasonably fitted by education, training, or experience, and after that time, only if his disability prevents him from performing the essential duties of his regular occupation
    (4) for an initial specified period, only if his disability prevents him from performing the essential duties of his regular occupation, and after that time, only if his disability prevents him from working at any occupation for which he is reasonably fitted by education, training, or experience

5. When Carlene Chadwick died, there were two conflicting claimants to her life insurance policy's death benefit. In order to resolve the conflict, the Cuyahoga Life Insurance Company used a legal remedy that is known as interpleader. In the United States, the use of interpleader in this situation indicates that Cuyahoga

   (1) paid the policy proceeds to both claimants in equal portions
   (2) reached an out-of-court compromise settlement with the claimants
   (3) paid the policy proceeds to Ms. Chadwick's estate and allowed the executor of the estate to distribute the proceeds according to the terms of Ms. Chadwick's will
   (4) paid the policy proceeds to a court and asked the court to decide the proper recipient

6. Some large employers with disabled employees have established vocational rehabilitation units that work closely with an insurer's claim examiners. The service that such a rehabilitation unit provides for individuals who have long-term disabilities is to

   (1) train these individuals to be self-employed
   (2) see that these individuals have opportunities to receive the therapy necessary to return to complete good health or to a productive occupation
   (3) retrain these individuals to do the work that they did before they became disabled
   (4) train these individuals to do work that may be entirely different from the work that they did before they became disabled

7. Stella Hollensteiner is insured by a medical expense insurance policy from the Knightsbridge Health Insurance Company. Her insurance policy has a 25 percent coinsurance provision and a $200 calendar year deductible. When Ms. Hollensteiner recently submitted a claim for $2,000 of eligible medical expenses, she had not met her deductible. Select the response that correctly identifies in the columns below the amount of expenses that, according to the terms of Ms. Hollensteiner's policy, Ms. Hollensteiner and Knightsbridge, respectively, will be required to pay.

	Ms. Hollensteiner	Knightsbridge
(1)	$500	$1,500
(2)	$650	$1,350
(3)	$700	$1,300
(4)	$1,550	$450

8. A coordination of benefits (COB) clause in a medical expense insurance policy attempts to resolve the problem of overinsurance. The purpose of a COB clause is to prevent an insured from

   (1) receiving insurance coverage from more than one medical expense insurance policy
   (2) receiving benefit payments that exceed the insured's total eligible medical expenses
   (3) receiving benefit payments for medical expenses that are excluded from payment in the medical expense insurance policy
   (4) obtaining new insurance coverage for pre-existing health problems which are known to the insured but not disclosed to the insurance company

9. The Grail Corporation offers its employees a medical expense insurance plan that contains a 30-day waiting period. In a medical expense insurance policy, the effect of such a waiting period is that

   (1) newly hired employees must be employed for at least 30 days before they become eligible for medical expense benefits
   (2) the insurance company can take up to 30 days to either deny or approve a claim
   (3) the policy does not cover the insured employees' medical expenses arising from sickness during the 30 days following the policy's issue
   (4) the policy does not cover the insured employees' medical expenses arising from accidents during the 30 days following the policy's issue

ANSWERS TO PRACTICE QUESTIONS

Chapter 11

(1) 1, pp. 308, 310
(2) 2, p. 304
(3) 3, p. 311
(4) 4, p. 320
(5) 4, pp. 311, 313

(6) 2, p. 322
(7) 2, pp. 315-16
(8) 2, pp. 316-17
(9) 3, pp. 314-15

SELF-RATING SCALE

If the number of correct answers is	Your knowledge of the chapter is
9	Excellent
8	Good
7	Fair
6	Marginal
5 or below	Unsatisfactory

PRACTICE QUESTIONS
Chapter 12

1. Sometimes the issuer of a security sells the issue directly to specific financial institutions, with or without the use of an investment banker, and therefore avoids the need to register the issue with government agencies. Such investment transactions are known as

    (1) spin-offs
    (2) public offerings
    (3) private placements
    (4) sale-and-leaseback transactions

2. From an investor's viewpoint, one characteristic that differentiates preferred stock from various other forms of investments is that preferred stock offers

    (1) greater certainty of income than do bonds
    (2) greater capital gains potential than does common stock
    (3) more voting rights than does common stock
    (4) greater preference in the distribution of a company's profits and assets than does common stock

3. The incorporated township of Polenta is issuing municipal bonds in order to raise money to build a toll road. The bonds are backed only by the income that the Polenta government expects to receive from operating the toll road. This information indicates that Polenta is issuing the type of bonds known as

    (1) unsecured bonds
    (2) corporate bonds
    (3) revenue bonds
    (4) general obligation bonds

4. Investment analysts use both bond ratings and bond yields as measures to evaluate bonds. A bond *yield* is expressed as a

    (1) letter grade and indicates the credit quality of the bond issue
    (2) letter grade and indicates the return the bond is expected to earn
    (3) ratio or percentage and indicates the credit quality of the bond issue
    (4) ratio or percentage and indicates the return the bond is expected to earn

5. Life and health insurance companies invest money in various types of assets — mortgages, stocks, bonds, and real estate. Of these categories of assets, the category in which most North American insurance companies hold the largest percentage of their assets is

    (1) mortgages
    (2) stocks
    (3) bonds
    (4) real estate

6. For investors, one advantage that real estate investments have over stocks is that *real estate* typically

    (1) represents equity ownership, whereas stocks do not
    (2) is a more liquid investment than are stocks
    (3) fluctuates more in value than do stocks
    (4) offers investors a higher rate of current income than do stocks

Questions 7 and 8 are matching questions. Items in the left-hand column are descriptions of types of preferred stocks. Choose the term from the right-hand column that matches each description.

7. Preferred stock which promises that the amount of any stated dividend which is not declared in one period must be added to the dividend due in the following period

8. Preferred stock that grants the holder the right to receive dividends above the stated rate if the issuing company has good earnings and declares an extra dividend

(1) A floating rate preferred stock

(2) A cumulative preferred stock

(3) A convertible preferred stock

(4) A participating preferred stock

* * * * * *

9. Government bonds can be general obligation bonds or revenue bonds. Of these types of government bonds, only *general obligation* bonds

    (1) are backed only by the credit and taxing power of the government unit that issued them
    (2) represent debt investments
    (3) are backed only by the income that the issuer expects to receive from the project that the bond issue supports
    (4) permit holders to sell a bond before its maturity date

10. The Delphinus Life and Health Insurance Company purchased real estate from a real estate developer as part of a sale-and-leaseback transaction. The effect of this transaction on Delphinus is that, as the lessor in the transaction, Delphinus

    (1) collects rental income directly from the property's tenants
    (2) maintains the property on a day-to-day basis
    (3) recovers the cost of the property's construction
    (4) obtains a sizable investment in a single income-producing real estate asset

11. Some bonds give the issuer the right to pay off the bonds at a specified price on a date earlier than the maturity date. Bonds that make this provision are said to be

    (1) convertible
    (2) cumulative
    (3) callable
    (4) participating

12. A collateralized mortgage obligation (CMO) is a type of

    (1) security that is backed by investments in mortgages
    (2) unsecured bond that is backed only by the full faith and credit of the issuer
    (3) mortgage that allows the interest rate to rise or fall with prevailing interest rates in the national economy
    (4) mortgage loan in which the borrower gradually pays off the loan by making periodic payments of principal and interest throughout the life of the mortgage

ANSWERS TO PRACTICE QUESTIONS
Chapter 12

(1) 3, pp. 344-45
(2) 4, p. 339
(3) 3, pp. 342, 344
(4) 4, p. 345
(5) 3, p. 342
(6) 4, p. 350

(7) 2, p. 339
(8) 4, p. 339
(9) 1, p. 342
(10) 4, pp. 352-53
(11) 3, p. 342
(12) 1, p. 349

SELF-RATING SCALE

If the number of correct answers is	Your knowledge of the chapter is
12	Excellent
11	Good
10	Fair
9	Marginal
8 or below	Unsatisfactory

PRACTICE QUESTIONS
Chapter 13

1. The Finnegan Press shipped $8,000 worth of books to the Retrograde Book Mart on an open-account basis. At the time of shipment, Finnegan's accountant recorded that Finnegan had sold $8,000 of merchandise, even though Finnegan may not receive a cash payment for another month. This information indicates that Finnegan uses the accounting system known as

    (1) accrual-basis accounting
    (2) advance and arrears accounting
    (3) cash-basis accounting
    (4) segregated accounting

2. The lock-box banking system is one method that insurers use to collect premium payments. In a lock-box banking system, premium payments are collected by the

    (1) insurer's sales agents, who collect premium payments at the homes of policyowners
    (2) policyowners, who administer their own insurance plans and prepare their own premium statements
    (3) insurer's bank, which opens premium payment envelopes and deposits the payments into the insurer's account
    (4) policyowners' banks, which transfer premium payments to the insurer's bank via computer networks

3. In the United States, insurers cannot include nonadmitted assets on the balance sheet of the Annual Statement. One category of nonadmitted assets consists of assets for which a portion of the value is admitted and the remainder of the value is nonadmitted. Most of the assets in this category are

    (1) office equipment
    (2) automobiles
    (3) computer software
    (4) investments

4. The financial condition of the Blackwater Company is represented in the following basic accounting equation:
$$\$28,500 = \$9,500 + \$19,000$$

    In this basic accounting equation, $28,500 represents Blackwater's total

    (1) assets
    (2) owner's equity
    (3) profit
    (4) liabilities

5. Canadian insurance companies that are registered under the Canadian and British Insurance Companies Act are required to file an Annual Statement with

    (1) the federal Department of Insurance and with each province in which the company is licensed to do business
    (2) only the federal Department of Insurance
    (3) only each province in which the company is licensed to do business
    (4) only the province in which the company's home office is located

6. The Neruda Life Insurance Company maintains a cash-basis accounting system. When Neruda receives premium payments for policies that have not yet been issued, Neruda's accountants record the payments in a temporary account. This temporary account is known as a

    (1) segregated account, and it is a type of asset account
    (2) suspense account, and it is a type of liability account
    (3) nonledger account, and it is a type of asset account
    (4) separate account, and it is a type of liability account

7. One type of expense budget for a life and health insurance company indicates the amount of money that the company expects to pay in the upcoming year for claims, cash surrenders, policy dividends, and policy loans. This type of expense budget is known as a

    (1) sales expense budget
    (2) benefits budget
    (3) capital expenditures budget
    (4) general and administrative expense budget

8. The following statement(s) can correctly be made about cash-basis accounting:

    A. Statutory accounting practices require that an insurance company's Annual Statement be presented on a cash basis
    B. In cash-basis accounting, journal entries are made only when cash actually changes hands
    C. Insurance companies maintain policy reserves on a cash basis

        (1) All of these
        (2) A and B only
        (3) A and C only
        (4) B only
        (5) C only

9. Typically, an accounting entry on the right side of a T-account for cash assets is

    (1) an advance
    (2) a debit
    (3) a credit
    (4) a loss

10. With respect to the auditing function in a life and health insurance company, it is correct to say that auditors typically

    (1) examine every operation and verify every financial transaction within a company
    (2) examine only those parts of a company's operations that directly involve the expenditure of funds
    (3) report whether a company's functions are carried out efficiently, but they do not make recommendations for improvement
    (4) rely on a system of statistical sampling in which they examine only a portion of a company's accounts, transactions, or operations

11. In the United States, the format and contents of an insurer's Annual Statement are specified by the

    (1) Society of Actuaries
    (2) state insurance commissioners
    (3) Securities and Exchange Commission
    (4) certified public accountants of life and health insurers

12. Life and health insurance companies maintain certain accounts separately from their general accounts. Such separate accounts (segregated accounts) are established in order to

    (1) manage the cash that is held for small disbursements
    (2) manage the funds that are used to support nonguaranteed insurance products
    (3) pay taxes on premium income
    (4) pay policy dividends to participating policyowners

13. Insurers must maintain some nonledger accounts to record certain assets and liabilities. One example of a nonledger account that would appear on an insurer's Annual Statement includes the insurer's

    (1) nonadmitted assets
    (2) cash disbursements for general operating expenses
    (3) policy reserves
    (4) payments of commissions to sales agents

ANSWERS TO PRACTICE QUESTIONS

Chapter 13

(1) 1, p. 371
(2) 3, p. 375
(3) 4, p. 373
(4) 1, p. 361
(5) 1, p. 370
(6) 2, pp. 371-72
(7) 2, p. 384

(8) 4, pp. 371-72
(9) 3, p. 363
(10) 4, p. 387
(11) 2, p. 367
(12) 2, pp. 378-79
(13) 3, p. 372

SELF-RATING SCALE

If the number of correct answers is	Your knowledge of the chapter is
13	Excellent
12	Good
11	Fair
10	Marginal
9 or below	Unsatisfactory

PRACTICE QUESTIONS
Chapter 14

1. Insurers typically try to resolve claim disputes before such disputes reach the stage of litigation. If litigation results from a claim dispute, and if the court rules in favor of the claimant, then the court may order the insurer to pay compensatory damages to the claimant. Compensatory damages include

    (1) contractual damages only
    (2) damages over and above the actual contract amount which are designed to punish the insurer for its behavior
    (3) contractual damages and also damages for a wrong that the insurer is found to have committed
    (4) the plaintiff's legal fees only

2. When hiring delivery truck drivers for its United States operations, the Hypersonic Delivery Service requires job applicants to meet certain height and weight requirements. These requirements are not justified by business necessity, nor are they a true test of a person's ability to perform the job. Hypersonic applies the height and weight requirements to men and women alike. Although Hypersonic's hiring practice appears to be neutral, it has the effect of disqualifying more women than men from employment. Because of this hiring practice, Hypersonic is engaging in the type of employment discrimination known as

    (1) equal employment discrimination
    (2) disparate impact discrimination
    (3) reverse employment discrimination
    (4) disparate treatment discrimination

3. Administrative law is one area of law within the legal departments of life and health insurance companies. One important duty within the area of administrative law would be

    (1) negotiating with labor unions to reach an agreement about working conditions for employees who are union members
    (2) seeking regulators' approval of items relating to insurance products, such as policy forms, rates, and advertising materials
    (3) advising an insurer's investment specialists about the best way to handle a particular real estate asset
    (4) drafting the agency agreements that an insurer and an agent enter into when the agent is hired

4. Bal Patel bought a life insurance policy from the Morgan Life Insurance Company. Because a life insurance policy is a unilateral contract, then in this situation, the right to maintain a suit against the other party for failure to fulfill a contractual promise would be available to

    (1) both Morgan Life and Mr. Patel
    (2) Morgan Life only
    (3) Mr. Patel only
    (4) neither Morgan Life nor Mr. Patel

5. A court in the United States determined that the Kilgallen Company had practiced employment discrimination against a former employee, Abraham Vargo. The court ordered Kilgallen to cease its discriminatory employment practices and to pay Mr. Vargo back pay. In this situation, *back pay* can be defined as

    (1) the legal fees that Mr. Vargo incurred in pursuing the lawsuit
    (2) damages for the emotional distress that Mr. Vargo suffered because of Kilgallen's discriminatory behavior
    (3) the wages and fringe benefits that Mr. Vargo would have received had he not been discriminated against
    (4) damages over and above the amount of Mr. Vargo's actual loss, and which are designed to punish Kilgallen for its discriminatory behavior

6. Gretchen Roth provides legal advice as outside counsel for the Barrington Life Insurance Company. This information indicates that Ms. Roth is a

    (1) lawyer who is a member of a private law firm
    (2) lawyer who is employed in one of Barrington's regional offices
    (3) lawyer who manages Barrington's home office legal department
    (4) paralegal who is employed in Barrington's home office legal department

7. In life and health insurance companies, the area of law that deals primarily with those sections of the tax code that specify the types of income that are taxable to individuals, as well as the expenditures that can be deducted from taxable income, is known as

    (1) estate tax law
    (2) corporate income tax law
    (3) real property law
    (4) personal income tax law

ANSWERS TO PRACTICE QUESTIONS

Chapter 14

(1) 3, p. 409
(2) 2, p. 403
(3) 2, p. 408
(4) 3, p. 398
(5) 3, p. 403
(6) 1, p. 393
(7) 4, p. 404

SELF-RATING SCALE

If the number of correct answers is	Your knowledge of the chapter is
7	Excellent
6	Good
5	Marginal
4 or below	Unsatisfactory

PRACTICE QUESTIONS
Chapter 15

1. Life and health insurance companies often use the point factor comparison system as a job evaluation method. The overall approach of the point factor comparison system is to evaluate

    (1) employees within a given job category and to rank them, from best to worst, based on specific characteristics of their work or behavior
    (2) the specific requirements and characteristics of each job within a company in order to establish wage and salary scales
    (3) the aptitude of entry-level clerical and technical-professional applicants who are seeking non-sales positions
    (4) the skills and knowledge of new employees in order to determine the training or development necessary for a new employee to fulfill specific job requirements

2. The Hampstead Life Insurance Company tests applicants for management positions by presenting the applicants with hypothetical work-related scenarios and then asking the applicants to respond accordingly. Applicants are evaluated on the basis of their response to various problems. This information indicates that the employment test which Hampstead administers to potential managers is an example of a

    A. Performance test
    B. Situation management test

    (1) Both A and B
    (2) A only
    (3) B only
    (4) Neither A nor B

3. Lynn Carlin, a human resources manager at the Cabell Life Insurance Company, wanted to calculate how many clerks Cabell's underwriting department needed to have on the job each day. Ms. Carlin divided the total number of insurance applications received in a typical day by the average number of applications that one underwriting clerk can screen in a day:

$$\frac{420 \text{ total applications per day}}{35 \text{ applications per clerk per day}} = 12$$

Ms. Carlin's result indicates that Cabell needs 12 clerks in the underwriting department each day. This information indicates that Ms. Carlin conducted a

    (1) skills inventory
    (2) trend analysis
    (3) case study
    (4) ratio analysis

4. In designing an employment application form, human resources professionals must avoid asking any questions that might lead to a charge of discrimination by an applicant who is not awarded a job. An example of an appropriate question to ask on the application form would be

    (1) "How old are you?"
    (2) "What is your church affiliation?"
    (3) "What was your salary at your last job?"
    (4) "Do you plan to get married in the future?"

5. The conference method is one common approach to training new employees. Essentially, the conference method consists of

   (1) placing trainees in small groups with a trainer present to provide feedback and guidance to the trainees as they generate solutions to problems
   (2) providing trainees with workbooks, computers, or other self-study devices that allow trainees to apply their knowledge of a subject
   (3) assigning some of the work and responsibility of a manager to a trainee, while the manager provides the trainee with instruction and encouragement
   (4) assigning a trainee to work with an experienced manager, with the goal of taking over the manager's job

6. The Crescent City Life and Health Insurance Company uses the same performance appraisal system for all of its employees. The form, illustrated below, lists four job-related characteristics which are assigned a rating from 1 for Marginal to 5 for Outstanding.

   Marginal----------------Outstanding

A. Completes work on time	1	2	3	4	5
B. Cooperates with fellow workers	1	2	3	4	5
C. Maintains high standards	1	2	3	4	5
D. Finds better ways to do work	1	2	3	4	5

   E. Overall score ____

   Crescent City's performance appraisal system is a type of

   (1) graphic rating scale
   (2) alternation ranking method
   (3) paired comparison method
   (4) behaviorally anchored rating scale

7. In order to be of value to an employer in selecting new employees, an employment test should be both valid and reliable. In the context of an employee selection test, *validity* refers to

   (1) whether a test is standardized so that it can be used by many different organizations without modification
   (2) the degree to which a test shows that applicants who do well on the test will also do well on the job
   (3) whether a test complies, as necessary, with relevant United States federal regulations or with the Canadian Provincial Human Rights Codes
   (4) the extent to which a test gives the same results on repeated administrations

8. Most life and health insurance companies recruit job candidates through both internal and external recruitment procedures. An example of an *internal* recruitment procedure would be a company's

   (1) paying bonuses to employees who refer job candidates who are hired
   (2) conducting job fairs at educational institutions
   (3) moving an employee from a position at one level in the company to another position at the same level of the hierarchy
   (4) identifying specialized technical staff through an executive search firm

9. The human resources department of the Volant Life and Health Insurance Company maintains a record that illustrates graphically the likely candidates for promotion to various key positions within Volant. In this record, several candidates are listed in order of preference under each position title. This record is known as a

    (1) position description
    (2) job posting
    (3) succession chart
    (4) skills inventory

10. Trend analysis is one technique that human resources professionals use to forecast employment levels. One characteristic of trend analysis, when used alone, is that trend analysis of employment levels

    (1) produces results that are more valid for small companies than for large companies
    (2) assumes that employment levels are affected by the passage of time only
    (3) measures how various factors, such as sales and technology, affect employment levels
    (4) is a qualitative, rather than a quantitative, forecasting technique

ANSWERS TO PRACTICE QUESTIONS

Chapter 15

(1) 2, p. 447
(2) 1, p. 431
(3) 4, p. 418
(4) 3, pp. 427, 430
(5) 1, p. 440

(6) 1, p. 443
(7) 2, p. 430
(8) 3, p. 423
(9) 3, p. 419
(10) 2, p. 418

SELF-RATING SCALE

If the number of correct answers is	Your knowledge of the chapter is
10	Excellent
9	Good
8	Fair
7	Marginal
6 or below	Unsatisfactory

PRACTICE QUESTIONS
Chapter 16

1. More and more insurance companies are converting their paper files to electronic images via image processing. When compared to the use of paper files, image processing typically

    (1) requires more storage space for documents
    (2) is less expensive to install
    (3) prevents several employees from having access to a document at the same time
    (4) improves the security of an insurance company's files

2. The information that insurers use can be classified as either operational information or management information, and it can come from either internal data or external data. Examples of information that insurers use routinely include lists of premium billings, account balances, and the amounts of agents' commissions. This information can be classified as

    (1) operational information and it comes from internal data
    (2) operational information and it comes from external data
    (3) management information and it comes from internal data
    (4) management information and it comes from external data

3. In a life and health insurance company, an underwriter would typically use an alpha system in order to

    (1) assess the effects of various underwriting impairments on the mortality of the company's policyowners
    (2) learn whether an applicant has other insurance coverage with the company
    (3) obtain information about an applicant from the Medical Information Bureau
    (4) produce policy pages containing rates and values as they will apply to an insurance policy

4. A well-designed data base enables an information system to provide operational and management information on a timely basis. In general, a data base is well-designed if the data is organized

    (1) so that each department's files are electronically separate from the files of other departments
    (2) into separate files or into related files that are connected through a master file
    (3) into one huge file that prevents several employees from using the same data simultaneously
    (4) so that each data item appears in a number of different files

5. Decision support systems provide important technical assistance to a company's employees. Typically, a decision support system for a life and health insurance company is designed to

    (1) make information accessible to managers so that managers can make informed decisions about the company's operations
    (2) make quick decisions or solve problems according to predetermined standards
    (3) record and process the daily transactions involved in administering insurance contracts
    (4) assist insurance prospects in making purchase decisions by illustrating how insurance products can be expected to perform under a variety of economic conditions and interest rate scenarios

6. The field offices of the Surrey Life Insurance Company use computer terminals to process information. The terminals can process information without being connected to the mainframe computer in Surrey's home office. This information indicates that the terminals in Surrey's field offices are known as

    (1) dumb terminals
    (2) modems
    (3) satellites
    (4) intelligent terminals

7. Whereas in a small insurance company only one person might perform the data administration function, a large company's information systems department would have a group of several workers performing the data administration function. Typically, the data administration function is responsible primarily for

    (1) writing computer programs
    (2) supervising the development of computer programs
    (3) scheduling and running jobs on the computer
    (4) implementing, maintaining, and controlling access to the corporate data bases

ANSWERS TO PRACTICE QUESTIONS

Chapter 16

(1) 4, p. 459
(2) 1, pp. 454-55
(3) 2, pp. 469-70
(4) 2, p. 456
(5) 1, p. 465
(6) 4, p. 458
(7) 4, p. 463

SELF-RATING SCALE

If the number of correct answers is	Your knowledge of the chapter is
7	Excellent
6	Good
5	Marginal
4 or below	Unsatisfactory

PRACTICE QUESTIONS

Chapters 17 and 18

1. A life insurance agent who encourages a client to replace a life insurance policy with another policy is acting within the law. Whether this action is also ethically acceptable depends on the reason for the replacement. An agent who encourages replacement only so that he or she can collect extra commissions is engaging in the unethical sales practice known as

    (1) twisting
    (2) churning
    (3) rebating
    (4) disintermediation

2. The Vigilant Life Insurance Company, which is domiciled in Canada, wanted to enter the life insurance business in Spain. In order to establish business in Spain, Vigilant joined forces with the DeSoto Life Insurance Company, which is domiciled in Spain. From DeSoto's viewpoint, one benefit of this joint venture is that

    (1) DeSoto is the single source of management control
    (2) joint ventures are exempt from government regulations
    (3) the risk involved in the joint venture is carried by Vigilant only
    (4) DeSoto can achieve a savings in overhead expenses as a result of combining operations with Vigilant

3. Host country staffing is one approach that insurers use to staff an international operation. One characteristic of host country staffing is that this approach to staffing a host country office usually

    (1) ensures that the culture of the host country's workplace will mesh with the home country's corporate culture
    (2) reduces the possibility of communication problems between home office personnel and host country staff
    (3) increases the insurer's risk of losing employees who do not adapt to the host country
    (4) has the overall effect of improving relations with the host country

4. In the country of Domingo, where the Lunar Life Insurance Company has just opened an office, it is the usual business custom for employees to take long midday breaks and then to work until late at night. In its home office in the United States, Lunar maintains office hours of 8:00 a.m. until 5:00 p.m. Lunar's managers will enforce these office hours in Domingo because they feel that, in general, United States managerial ideas and policies are superior to those of Domingo. In this situation, Lunar's managerial attitude toward international operations can be described as

    (1) an ethnocentric attitude
    (2) a polycentric attitude
    (3) a matrix attitude
    (4) a geocentric attitude

5. Ethical behavior is behavior in accordance with accepted principles of right and wrong. One characteristic of ethical principles is that they

    (1) are identical throughout the world
    (2) apply to individuals, but never to organizations
    (3) are always applied uniformly in judging behavior
    (4) vary from one group to another, according to the values of each group

6. When conducting business in international markets, insurers must consider the same marketing concerns as they do when conducting business in domestic markets. Specifically, insurers must consider the "four Ps" of marketing: product, pricing, place, and

    (1) people
    (2) profitability
    (3) promotion
    (4) persistency

7. When deciding whether to operate on an international basis, an insurer will consider the potential benefits and drawbacks of international operations. Only one of the following statements about the international operations of life and health insurance companies is false.

    A. Foreign countries provide an insurer with the chance to test new marketing strategies and techniques before using them in the insurer's home country
    B. By operating in a greater number of countries, an insurer achieves greater concentration of its political risk
    C. An insurer can realize lower costs of producing business overseas because its fixed costs of operating the entire business are spread over a larger customer base
    D. In a foreign market, an insurer may be able to offer a life insurance product that, because of legal constraints, cannot be sold domestically

    Of statements A, B, C, and D, the **FALSE** statement is

    (1) A
    (2) B
    (3) C
    (4) D

8. The following statement(s) can correctly be made about the importance of corporate ethics:

    A. A company that desires close relationships with its customers must act ethically to avoid damaging relationships based on trust and good faith
    B. If a company asks its employees to do something unethical or if it tolerates unethical behavior, it risks undermining its employees' motivation and trust

       (1) Both A and B
       (2) A only
       (3) B only
       (4) Neither A nor B

ANSWERS TO PRACTICE QUESTIONS

Chapters 17 and 18

(1) 2, c. 18, p. 502
(2) 4, c. 17, p. 490
(3) 4, c. 17, p. 494
(4) 1, c. 17, p. 478

(5) 4, c. 18, pp. 501-02
(6) 3, c. 17, p. 496
(7) 2, c. 17, pp. 483-85
(8) 1, c. 18, p. 502

SELF-RATING SCALE

If the number of correct answers is	Your knowledge of the chapter is
8	Excellent
7	Good
6	Marginal
5 or below	Unsatisfactory

Practice Test

This section consists of a full, 75-question practice test. The internal directions are the same as you can expect to encounter when you sit for your examination, except that any reference to an answer sheet is omitted in the practice test. In addition, the practice test does not contain a cover sheet that is standard with the regular examinations.

The questions appearing in the practice test appear in standard formats utilized in the FLMI examinations. Considered in its totality, the practice test incorporates the same mix of question types and difficulties as you can expect to see in the examination for which you sit. Of course, you should not expect to see any of the questions appearing in the practice test in the examination that you will take.

The practice test represents a very close approximation to the level of test difficulty that you can expect to encounter when you sit for your examination. Since its question mix is also representative, the practice test provides you with a good opportunity to approximate your overall level of preparation for the regular examination. Your overall score on the practice test should be within three points, plus or minus, of the score that you could reasonably expect to achieve with the same level of preparation on the regular examination.

You should take the practice test only after you have completed your study with the textbook, the Student Guide, and the practice questions in this publication.

Write the number of your chosen response to the left of the question number in the practice test. At the end of the practice test is an answer key and text references list. You should avoid consulting the answer key and text references list until you have completed the practice test. Put yourself in a realistic test-room situation, allowing yourself up to two, or even three, hours to answer all the questions, using the test-taking methodology outlined in the introduction to this guide. Then grade your responses according to the answer key. Using the textbook and text references, look up the answers to any questions you answered incorrectly.

If your overall score on the practice test is only marginal, you have a reasonably reliable indication of the need for more review. After all, given the representative difficulty level of the practice test, it is unwise to believe that there will be a radically different result on the regular examination. Use whatever preparation time remaining to you before the regular examination to bolster your chances of passing, and even of making a perfect score.

This examination contains 75 questions.

These questions include multiple-choice questions, matching questions, and multiple-statement questions. Each question is valued at 1 1/3 points.

Multiple-choice questions require you to complete a statement. Alongside the corresponding question number on your Answer Sheet, darken the space containing the number of the choice that most accurately completes the statement.

Matching questions require you to match a term or statement in one column with a term or statement in another column. Instructions for answering these questions appear with each set of matching questions.

Multiple-statement questions require you to choose the response that correctly and most completely meets the requirements of the introduction. The introduction is followed by several statements or terms labeled A, B, etc., which are in turn followed by a series of responses numbered (1), (2), (3), etc. Determine whether each statement or term meets the requirements of the introduction; then select the numbered response that contains the letter(s) you have chosen.

1. In one approach to selling insurance, a life insurance agent isolates a particular financial need of a prospect and tries to meet that need with an insurance product that is suited for the purpose. This sales method is known as

    (1) single-need selling
    (2) estate planning
    (3) conservation
    (4) total-needs programming

2. The Whitemarsh Life Insurance Company maintains a computerized data base of information about the education, work experience, and special qualifications of Whitemarsh's employees. Whitemarsh uses this information to identify employees and their qualifications for various positions in the company. This information indicates that Whitemarsh maintains a

    (1) succession chart
    (2) skills inventory
    (3) point factor comparison system
    (4) graphic rating scale

3. In contrast to direct mail advertising, one advantage that *print media* advertising typically offers to a marketer is the ability to

    (1) reach a more specifically defined audience
    (2) achieve a lower cost per person exposed to the advertising
    (3) achieve higher response rates
    (4) segment a target market according to a wider range of demographic variables

4. In 1819, United States Supreme Court Chief Justice John Marshall defined a certain form of business as "an artificial being, invisible, intangible, and existing only in contemplation of the law." This definition refers to

    (1) sole proprietorships
    (2) partnerships
    (3) strategic alliances
    (4) corporations

5. Ruth Hidell holds 50 shares of common stock in the Marina Life Insurance Company. Ms. Hidell also owns two life insurance policies issued by the Knoll Life Insurance Company, which is a mutual insurance company. Both Marina Life and Knoll Life are in the process of holding elections for their board of directors. Ms. Hidell possesses certain voting rights as a common stockholder with Marina Life and as a policyowner of Knoll Life.

   Select the response that correctly identifies in the columns below the number of votes that Ms. Hidell is eligible to cast in the elections of Marina Life and Knoll Life, respectively.

	Marina Life	Knoll Life
(1)	1 vote	1 vote
(2)	1 vote	2 votes
(3)	50 votes	1 vote
(4)	50 votes	2 votes

6. The Underhill Life Insurance Company, domiciled in the United States, joined forces with the Iqbal Life Insurance Company, domiciled in Pakistan, for the purpose of entering the life insurance market in Pakistan. From Underhill Life's viewpoint, one benefit of this joint venture is that

   (1) the risk involved in the venture is carried by Iqbal Life only
   (2) Underhill Life is the single source of management control
   (3) Underhill Life is exempt from Pakistan's government regulations
   (4) working with Iqbal Life can reduce the chances of making social or linguistic mistakes with the consumers in Pakistan

7. In the United States, life and health insurance companies cannot admit certain assets on the balance sheets of their Annual Statements. Some assets are categorized as nonadmitted because

   (1) ownership of such assets is a threat to the financial solvency of life and health insurance companies
   (2) the realizable value of such assets is uncertain
   (3) life and health insurance companies are legally prohibited from owning such assets
   (4) they are reserved to pay future claims on in-force life and health insurance policies

8. Generally, for group insurance coverage, the insurer's antiselection risk tends to be minimized if

   (1) a group is small
   (2) individual members of a group are allowed to choose the amount of their insurance protection
   (3) a group insurance plan is noncontributory
   (4) a group is formed for the purpose of purchasing insurance coverage

9. Red Clay Landscaping, a small company with 20 employees, is transferring its group life insurance coverage to a new carrier, the Legerity Life Insurance Group. In determining Red Clay's initial premium rates, Legerity Life will rely more strongly on

   (1) manual rates, which are based on the mortality experience of an average group, rather than relying on experience rates
   (2) manual rates, which are based on Red Clay's own prior claim experience, rather than relying on blended rates
   (3) experience rates, which are based on the mortality experience of an average group, rather than relying on manual rates
   (4) blended rates, which are based on Red Clay's own prior claim experience, rather than relying on manual rates

Questions 10 and 11 are matching questions. In the left-hand column are descriptions of various discriminatory employment practices that are prohibited by United States law. From the right-hand column, select the answer that matches each description.

10. An employment policy that appears to be neutral but that results in a disproportionately negative effect on a group of people who are protected by law

11. The intentional discrimination against certain people because of race, color, religion, sex, age, or national origin

(1) Perpetuation of past discrimination

(2) Disparate treatment

(3) Internal job posting

(4) Disparate impact

* * * * * *

12. State and provincial laws allow for the revocation of an insurance agent's license for engaging in certain prohibited sales practices. One such prohibited practice is called *twisting*. Twisting consists of an agent's

    (1) offering the purchaser a share in the agent's sales commission
    (2) offering to reinstate a lapsed policy, without first obtaining new evidence of insurability, by simply accepting renewal premiums after the grace period has expired
    (3) attempting to prevent the lapse of a policy that the agent had sold, in an effort to preserve the renewal commissions
    (4) making false or misleading statements to the disadvantage of the policyowner about the value of an existing policy in order to induce the policyowner to change insurers

13. As a branch manager for a field office of the Carousel Life Insurance Company, Candice Rubenstein's job consists of recruiting, training, and motivating the field office's soliciting agents. Carousel's contract and compensation practices are typical of the branch office system. This information indicates that the soliciting agents in the field office are under contract to

    (1) Carousel, and Carousel provides the funds to pay for sales commissions
    (2) Carousel, and Ms. Rubenstein provides the funds to pay for sales commissions
    (3) Ms. Rubenstein, and Carousel provides the funds to pay for sales commissions
    (4) Ms. Rubenstein, and Ms. Rubenstein provides the funds to pay for sales commissions

14. In order to earn an interest rate higher than the rate her individual life insurance policy was yielding, Rachel Borensky surrendered her life insurance policy and invested its cash value in a certificate of deposit. Ms. Borensky's financial transaction is an example of

    (1) churning
    (2) deregulation
    (3) disintermediation
    (4) movement of securities

15. Yuri Pavel and Ken O'Donnell are employees in the information systems department of the Elm Life Insurance Company. Mr. Pavel recently designed a new computer system to meet Elm Life's operational needs. After Mr. Pavel developed a computerized solution to Elm Life's problems, he communicated the solution to Mr. O'Donnell, who then translated the solution into a functioning program. This information indicates that Mr. Pavel's and Mr. O'Donnell's jobs, respectively, are that of

    (1) input clerk and output clerk
    (2) computer operator and data administrator
    (3) systems analyst and programmer
    (4) programmer/analyst and end user

16. Actuaries gather statistics in order to calculate premiums and reserves for life and health insurance products. Continuance tables provide actuaries with

    (1) mortality statistics that present the probabilities of living and dying for a large group of people
    (2) standard premium rates that were developed independently of the mortality experience of any particular group
    (3) conservative assumptions about the levels of interest that insurance companies can expect to earn on investments
    (4) morbidity statistics that indicate the distribution of claims according to the duration of the illness or to the amount of expense involved in the claims

17. In order to incorporate through the federal government, a Canadian insurance company must petition the appropriate government agency for incorporation through the use of

    (1) a memorandum of association
    (2) a corporate charter
    (3) letters patent
    (4) an ethical code

18. The major functional areas in a life and health insurance company include the marketing, actuarial, accounting, and legal departments. Each of these areas can be classified as being either a line unit or a staff unit. Select the response that correctly identifies for each column whether a given functional area is a line unit or a staff unit.

	Marketing	Actuarial	Accounting	Legal
(1)	line	staff	staff	staff
(2)	staff	line	staff	line
(3)	line	line	staff	staff
(4)	line	staff	line	line

19. Within life and health insurance companies, accounting personnel sometimes maintain suspense accounts for the purpose of

    (1) recording cash receipts that cannot be credited immediately to a permanent account
    (2) allocating funds for significant purchases and acquisitions
    (3) recording assets and liabilities that are not affected by cash transactions
    (4) investing the funds from nonguaranteed insurance products without affecting the funds in general accounts

20. For sales presentation purposes, life insurance agents commonly use a computer system that allows them to input variables on a case-by-case basis. This type of information system is essential to showing a prospect how an investment-based life insurance product will perform under a variety of economic conditions and interest rate scenarios, and with premium payments of various amounts. Such an information system is known as

    (1) a new business system
    (2) a daily cycle system
    (3) an alpha system
    (4) a ledger proposal system

21. For health insurers in the United States, health maintenance organizations (HMOs) have emerged as a mechanism for providing health care. One characteristic of HMOs is that they

    (1) emphasize maintaining the good health of their members
    (2) have little economic incentive to reduce health care costs
    (3) are ineligible for any form of federal sponsorship
    (4) exclude routine preventive procedures, such as annual checkups, from the services they provide to members

22. When interviewing potential customer service representatives, the Rosetta Life Insurance Company presents applicants with various hypothetical, work-related situations and asks the applicants to respond accordingly. Rosetta then evaluates applicants on the basis of their responses. This information indicates that, when selecting customer service representatives, Rosetta uses the type of employment test known as

    (1) an aptitude test
    (2) a personality test
    (3) a situation management test
    (4) an integrity test

23. Marcia Livesley is being trained in the accounting department of the Bachman Mutual Insurance Company. Every week Ms. Livesley moves from one accounting job to another, so that she develops a complete understanding of each accounting function. Thus, Ms. Livesley performs a variety of tasks without her job's increasing in complexity at any one time. This information indicates that the training which Ms. Livesley is receiving can be described as

    A. Job rotation
    B. On-the-job training

       (1) Both A and B
       (2) A only
       (3) B only
       (4) Neither A nor B

24. In 1980, the Pershing Insurance Company was incorporated in the state of Indiana. Pershing later applied for and was granted permission to do business in the states of Michigan and Illinois. In 1992, Pershing moved its home office from Indiana to the state of Illinois. Pershing is said to be *domiciled* in

    A. Indiana
    B. Michigan
    C. Illinois

       (1) All of these
       (2) B and C only
       (3) A only
       (4) C only

25. By operating in a number of countries, a life and health insurance company is diversifying its

    A. Underwriting risk
    B. Economic risk
    C. Political risk

       (1) All of these
       (2) A and B only
       (3) B and C only
       (4) A only
       (5) C only

26. Accountants use T-accounts to record transactions involving assets, liabilities, and owners' equity items. The effect of a *debit* entered in a T-account is

    (1) an increase in asset, expense, liability, income, and owners' equity accounts
    (2) a decrease in asset, expense, liability, income, and owners' equity accounts
    (3) an increase in liability, income, and owners' equity accounts, but a decrease in asset and expense accounts
    (4) an increase in asset and expense accounts, but a decrease in liability, income, and owners' equity accounts

27. How an insurer staffs an international operation usually depends on whether the insurer follows an ethnocentric, a geocentric, or a polycentric approach. If following a *polycentric* approach to staffing an international operation, an insurer will staff the host country's workplace with

    (1) staff members from the home country
    (2) citizens of the host country
    (3) the best available people, regardless of nationality
    (4) third-country nationals

28. The Camp Life Insurance Company uses the numerical rating system to assign proposed life insureds to risk classes. Camp uses 100 as the basic rating value. Camp assigned the following ratings to Josephine Milteer on her application for life insurance:

Factor	Rating	
	Debit	Credit
Basic Rating	100	
Build	30	
Girth		10
Family history		20
Subtotal	130	30

    This information indicates that Camp has assigned Ms. Milteer a total numerical rating of

    (1) 100 points, and that Ms. Milteer will be assigned to a standard risk class
    (2) 100 points, and that Ms. Milteer will be assigned to a substandard risk class
    (3) 160 points, and that Ms. Milteer will be assigned to a standard risk class
    (4) 160 points, and that Ms. Milteer will be assigned to a substandard risk class

29. If a company produces only one product and defines the total market for that product as its target market, then that company is following the target market strategy known as

    (1) differentiated marketing
    (2) concentrated marketing
    (3) test marketing
    (4) undifferentiated marketing

30. When processing a life or health insurance claim, claim examiners typically determine if the person suffering the loss was actually covered under the insurance policy. During this stage of the claim decision process, the majority of problems encountered by examiners result from

    (1) claimants' making unintentional mistakes
    (2) claimants' intentionally using false information in an attempt to collect policy benefits
    (3) claims that require extensive investigation in order to verify all of the relevant information
    (4) claims filed under insurance policies that were not in force at the time of loss

31. The following statements are about job changes involving various employees of a life insurance company. Decide which of these individuals made a lateral transfer.

    A. Karen Arnold moved from her position as a Human Resources Assistant to the higher position of a Human Resources Associate
    B. Dee Bucknell moved from her position as an administrative assistant in the marketing department to the equal position of an administrative assistant in the underwriting department
    C. Tad Calloway was moved from his position as a Claims Administration Manager to the lower position of a Claims Administration Specialist
    D. Jake Delgado learned electronic publishing so that he could better perform his work as a Corporate Communications Assistant

    This information indicates that the individual who made a lateral transfer is

    (1) Ms. Arnold
    (2) Ms. Bucknell
    (3) Mr. Calloway
    (4) Mr. Delgado

32. The following statements are about product design requirements that a life insurance policy must meet. Only one of these statements does not represent the consumer's viewpoint.

    A. The policy must provide benefits that meet the consumer's needs
    B. The premium to be charged for the coverage must be competitive in the marketplace
    C. The policy must be profitable to the life insurance company
    D. The cost of the policy's coverage must be within the consumer's financial means

    Of statements A, B, C, and D, the statement that does **NOT** represent the consumer's viewpoint is

    (1) A
    (2) B
    (3) C
    (4) D

33. The following statements are about group life insurance policies. Only one of these statements is false.

    A. The majority of these policies are issued as one-year renewable term insurance
    B. The individuals insured under these policies are actual parties to the master contracts
    C. The majority of groups insured under these policies are employer-employee groups
    D. Interest is usually a more important factor in the calculation of premium rates for individual life insurance policies than for these policies

    Of statements A, B, C, and D, the **FALSE** statement is

    (1) A
    (2) B
    (3) C
    (4) D

34. When underwriting life insurance, insurance companies consider many factors that affect the degree of mortality risk presented by a proposed life insured. The following statements are about risk factors for life insurance. Only one of these statements is true.

    A. A person who is significantly overweight represents the same mortality risk as a person of average weight
    B. Flying as a fare-paying passenger on regularly scheduled airline flights is sufficiently hazardous to increase a person's mortality risk
    C. A proposed insured's family history is usually considered an important factor if it reflects a characteristic that also appears in some form in the proposed insured
    D. The majority of rated life insurance policies are rated because of nonmedical, rather than medical, risk factors

    Of statements A, B, C, and D, the **TRUE** statement is

    (1) A
    (2) B
    (3) C
    (4) D

35. If a corporation fails and its assets are sold to raise money to pay its debts, certain investors' claims on the business will be paid before the claims of other investors. A corporation's investors can include

    A. Bondholders
    B. Common stockholders
    C. Preferred stockholders

    Beginning with the investors having the *highest* claim priority and ending with the investors having the lowest claim priority, the order in which these claims must be satisfied is

    (1) A—B—C
    (2) A—C—B
    (3) B—C—A
    (4) C—B—A

36. Actuaries at the Aspen Life and Health Insurance Company constructed a table to express the lapse and persistency rates for a particular block of life insurance policies. Consider the following portion of their lapse table:

Policy Year	Number of Policies Persisting	Number of Policies Lapsing
1	2,000	500

    This information indicates that, during Policy Year 1, this particular block of policies had a lapse rate of

    (1) 25 percent, and a persistency rate of 25 percent
    (2) 25 percent, and a persistency rate of 75 percent
    (3) 75 percent, and a persistency rate of 25 percent
    (4) 75 percent, and a persistency rate of 75 percent

37. Jet screening, which is a part of the underwriting process in many life and health insurance companies, occurs when

    (1) underwriting personnel quickly decline or rate the applications of proposed insureds with significant health problems
    (2) home office personnel verify with the Medical Information Bureau that medical information on applications is complete
    (3) soliciting agents gather pertinent information about proposed insureds that could influence the risk selection decision
    (4) underwriting personnel process proposed insureds' applications as quickly as possible

38. The Solstice Life Insurance Company divides its operations into two segments of business — Group Life and Individual Life. Each of these segments controls its own revenues and expenses, and makes its own decisions regarding its operations. Solstice's word processing department provides support services to both the Group Life and the Individual Life segments. Within Solstice's organizational structure, both Solstice's Group Life and its Individual Life operations can be classified as

    (1) profit centers, and the word processing department can be classified as a service center
    (2) service centers, and the word processing department can be classified as a subsidiary
    (3) matrix organizations, and the word processing department can be classified as a revenue center
    (4) resource centers, and the word processing department can be classified as a strategic business unit

39. When there are conflicting claimants to a life insurance policy's benefits, a life insurance company can pay the policy proceeds to a court so that the court can determine the proper recipient of the policy's benefits. In the United States, this legal remedy is known as

    (1) rescission
    (2) interpleader
    (3) coordination of benefits
    (4) absolute assignment

40. One approach to employee performance appraisals is the essay appraisal technique. One drawback of using this technique is that, in the essay appraisal technique,

    (1) an employee's evaluation often relies upon the appraiser's ability to write clearly
    (2) the structured form limits the appraiser's ability to evaluate all employees with the same criteria
    (3) the appraiser is required to focus on isolated incidents relating to an employee's performance, rather than on day-to-day activities
    (4) the appraiser has little flexibility to indicate or to weight various aspects of an employee's performance

41. Marie Moorman wanted to have cosmetic surgery, but she discovered that the expense was not covered under her group medical expense insurance contract. This information indicates that, in Ms. Moorman's medical expense insurance contract, cosmetic surgery is identified as

    (1) a deductible
    (2) an exclusion
    (3) a pre-existing condition
    (4) an impairment

42. The Bertrand Corporation's group health insurance contract with the Dauphine Health Insurance Company contains a conversion privilege. This information indicates that, if Bertrand terminates its group insurance contract with Dauphine, Dauphine's customer service department will

    (1) transfer the files for Bertrand's contract to Bertrand's new group health insurer
    (2) maintain the files for Bertrand's contract for at least one year, so that Bertrand can reactivate its contract if so desired
    (3) close the files for Bertrand's contract and inform Bertrand's eligible group members of their right to convert their group insurance coverage into individual insurance coverage
    (4) close the files for Bertrand's contract and allow Bertrand's group members to apply for individual insurance policies with greater amounts of coverage than in their group plan

43. One **TRUE** statement about the cross-selling of insurance products is that the cross-selling approach

    (1) increases the amount of prospecting necessary to generate new business
    (2) is made possible by the multiple-line agency (MLA) system
    (3) results in a lower-than-average total premium per customer
    (4) reflects the insurance industry's movement from a customer-centered orientation to a more product-centered approach to business

44. Actuaries are predicting the annual claim cost for a block of one-year surgical expense policies for 1,000 women who are 40 years old. The actuaries predict that 100 of these women will file a claim, and that the average claim will be for $800. This information indicates that the predicted annual claim cost for this block of policies is

    (1) $80,000, and the net one-year term premium for one of these policies is $80
    (2) $80,000, and the net one-year term premium for one of these policies is $100
    (3) $800,000, and the net one-year term premium for one of these policies is $800
    (4) $800,000, and the net one-year term premium for one of these policies is $1,000

45. In the later years of a level-premium life insurance policy, the total amount of net premiums collected is less than the future amount of expected claims. To account for the excess premiums received under the level premium system, a life insurance company will establish an account that identifies the money that the insurance company must pay in future claims. This account is known as the

    (1) loading
    (2) policy reserve
    (3) contingency fund
    (4) contribution to surplus

46. Coordination is a concept that is fundamental to the management of business organizations. In the context of management, coordination is defined as the

    (1) obligation that an employee has to perform assigned duties
    (2) belief that employees are answerable for how well they use their authority and handle their responsibility for achieving goals
    (3) right of an employee to make decisions, take action, and direct others in order to complete assigned duties
    (4) orderly arrangement of a company's activities so that the company's goals can be achieved

47. Many life and health insurers collect premiums through methods other than sending notices and waiting for payment. Under a lock-box banking system for collecting premiums, the

    (1) insurer's bank opens premium payment envelopes and deposits the payments to the insurer's account
    (2) policyowner authorizes the insurer to withdraw future premiums from the policyowner's savings or checking account
    (3) policyowner's bank transfers premium payments to the insurer's bank via computers
    (4) insurer's soliciting agents collect premiums from policyowners at their homes

48. Consider the following financial data from the Prouty Company's balance sheet:

    Assets $180,000
    Liabilities $135,000
    Capital .... $ 45,000

    This information indicates that, for the Prouty Company, the basic accounting equation can be expressed as

    (1) $180,000 + $135,000 + $45,000
    (2) $180,000 ($135,000 - $45,000)
    (3) $180,000 = $135,000 + $45,000
    (4) $180,000 ÷ ($135,000 + $45,000)

49. The Dante Life Insurance Company has a facultative reinsurance treaty with the Banister Reinsurance Company. In accordance with the terms of a facultative treaty, Banister Re will

    (1) rely solely on the accuracy of Dante Life's risk selection
    (2) make an independent underwriting decision on each risk sent to it by Dante Life
    (3) provide reinsurance coverage on an insured even if the insured dies before Dante Life notifies Banister Re that the risk has been ceded
    (4) provide reinsurance for all coverage amounts in excess of Dante Life's retention limit

50. A life or health insurance policy is a unilateral contract because legally enforceable promises are made by

    (1) both the insurer and the policyowner
    (2) the insurer only
    (3) the policyowner only
    (4) neither the insurer nor the policyowner

51. Julia Mercer contacted the Warren Life Insurance Company upon discovering that her name was misspelled as Julie Mercer on her new individual life insurance policy. This information indicates that Warren Life's customer service department would correct the error by

    (1) reissuing the current insurance policy with the correct spelling of Ms. Mercer's name
    (2) requiring Ms. Mercer to undergo the entire application process once again
    (3) requiring Ms. Mercer to return the insurance policy so that Warren Life could attach an endorsement
    (4) declaring that Ms. Mercer's life insurance policy was void from its inception

52. Marguerite Dahl, a customer service manager for the Benbrook Assurance Company, divided the total number of calls received each evening by the number of inquiries that one customer service representative can handle in one evening:

$$\frac{200 \text{ total calls per evening}}{50 \text{ calls per representative per evening}} = \frac{4}{1}$$

From this calculation, Ms. Dahl determined that Benbrook needed four customer service representatives in the office each evening. This information indicates that Ms. Dahl conducted a

(1) ratio analysis, which is a quantitative forecasting technique
(2) trend analysis, which is a quantitative forecasting technique
(3) ratio analysis, which is a qualitative forecasting technique
(4) trend analysis, which is a qualitative forecasting technique

53. In data communications networks, telephone lines can be used to transmit data from one point to another through a transmission link. In such a network, both the sending unit and the receiving unit must be attached to a device called

(1) a modem
(2) a satellite
(3) a dumb terminal
(4) an intelligent terminal

54. When the Fletcher Life Insurance Company first invested in a mortgage, the mortgage loan was yielding an interest rate of 6 percent. Five years later, the interest rate on Fletcher Life's mortgage loan rose to 10 percent to reflect prevailing interest rates in the national economy. This information indicates that Fletcher Life is holding the type of mortgage loan known as

(1) a mortgage-backed security
(2) a collateralized mortgage obligation
(3) an adjustable-rate mortgage
(4) a pass-through certificate

55. With respect to risk classification for life insurance, it is correct to say that life insurers typically

(1) offer standard premium rates to preferred risks
(2) offer substandard rates to the majority of applicants for ordinary life insurance
(3) use industry-wide standards, rather than their own standards, for classifying risks
(4) divide impaired risks in the substandard risk class into several substandard classes

56. Customers of a life and health insurance company generally fall into four major categories: policyowners/insureds, soliciting agents, beneficiaries, and account holders. From a life and health insurance company's viewpoint, the customers who are considered to be both internal and external customers are the company's

(1) policyowners/insureds
(2) soliciting agents
(3) beneficiaries
(4) account holders

57. When evaluating a potential investment, a life and health insurance company will consider the ease with which the investment can be converted into cash quickly and at a reasonable price. This characteristic of investments is known as

    (1) diversification
    (2) expected rate of return
    (3) yield
    (4) liquidity

58. Certain associations in the United States and Canada develop model insurance legislation and promote uniformity in insurance regulations. In the United States and in Canada, respectively, these associations are the

    (1) state insurance departments and the Privy Council
    (2) Securities and Exchange Commission and the Office of the Superintendent of Financial Institutions
    (3) Internal Revenue Service and the Association of Superintendents of Insurance
    (4) National Association of Insurance Commissioners and the Canadian Council of Insurance Regulators

59. Somerset Manufacturers records its income items when they are earned and records its expense items when they are incurred, regardless of whether cash has actually been received or spent. Thus, Somerset uses the accounting system known as

    (1) advance and arrears accounting
    (2) cash-basis accounting
    (3) segregated accounting
    (4) accrual-basis accounting

60. In determining the extra premium amount to charge a proposed life insured who is classified as a substandard risk, life insurers typically

    (1) develop a specific extra premium amount for the proposed insured's particular impairment
    (2) predict the longevity of the proposed insured and charge a premium amount accordingly
    (3) assume that a hazard leading to the proposed insured's substandard risk classification can be classified on the basis of whether, over time, the hazard will increase, decrease, or remain the same
    (4) impose a probationary period to determine whether, over time, the hazard leading to the proposed insured's substandard risk classification will increase, decrease, or remain the same

61. One component of an information system ensures that the system performs according to specifications and that the system operates under necessary levels of security. This component is called

    (1) input
    (2) output
    (3) processing
    (4) control

62. Edward Chung is a personal producing general agent (PPGA) who sells life and health insurance products. If Mr. Chung is typical of other PPGAs operating under the PPGA distribution system, then he

    (1) holds an exclusive contract with one insurance company
    (2) works out of an insurance company's field office
    (3) spends most of his time managing a life and health insurance agency
    (4) works alone and engages primarily in prospecting and sales

63. The probability that predicted results will match actual results increases with the number of observations that are made. This concept, which actuaries use to predict mortality rates, is known as

    (1) retrocession
    (2) the going-concern concept
    (3) economies of scale
    (4) the law of large numbers

64. Renate Olsen, the manager of a life insurance company's field agency, is preparing the part of the agency's operating plan that forecasts the levels of new and renewal business that the agency expects to produce, as well as forecasts of the agency's operating expenses. This part of an agency's operating plan is known as

    (1) a compensation schedule
    (2) an expense ratio
    (3) an operating budget
    (4) a functional cost analysis

65. Garrison Shaw, a product design actuary with a life insurance company, conducted an asset share calculation on a new participating life insurance product. After studying the results of the asset share calculation, Mr. Shaw determined that the validation period, or the amount of time in which the product would become profitable, was too long. One product design change that Mr. Shaw can make to shorten the validation period is to

    (1) decrease the product's gross premium
    (2) increase the product's cash values
    (3) decrease the product's dividends
    (4) increase the product's expense rate

66. A number of internal and external factors in the business environment affect a life and health insurance company's marketing plan. *External* factors include the company's

    (1) existing products
    (2) competitors
    (3) current distribution systems
    (4) financial condition

67. The two basic types of accounting principles are statutory accounting practices (SAP) and generally accepted accounting principles (GAAP). In the United States, life and health insurance companies typically prepare their Annual Statements and annual reports as follows:

	Annual Statements	Annual reports
(1)	SAP	SAP
(2)	GAAP	SAP
(3)	SAP	GAAP
(4)	GAAP	GAAP

68. The various investments that insurers typically hold can be classified as stocks, bonds, mortgages, and real estate. Life and health insurance companies in the United States and Canada hold the largest percentage of their assets in the form of investments in

    (1) stocks
    (2) bonds
    (3) mortgages
    (4) real estate

69. As an employee of the Beverly Life Insurance Company, Oliver Duran administers the stock area of the investment department. Mr. Duran evaluates investment opportunities and he makes Beverly's day-to-day decisions about stock investing. Beverly is required to follow the prudent investor rule when investing policyowners' money. With respect to Mr. Duran's position with Beverly and to the mandates of the prudent investor rule, this information indicates that Mr. Duran is

    (1) a portfolio manager, and Beverly must exercise sound and reasoned judgment in making its investment decisions
    (2) an asset manager, and Beverly must hold no more than 10 percent of its assets in common stock
    (3) a registered representative, and Beverly must exercise sound and reasoned judgment in making its investment decisions
    (4) an investment analyst, and Beverly must hold no more than 10 percent of its assets in common stock

70. A life and health insurance company's organization chart can be outlined in the shape of a pyramid. A company's owners usually are not shown on the organization chart because they do not direct the actual operations of the company. In actuality, the top of a typical pyramidal organization chart is occupied by a company's

    (1) vice presidents
    (2) board of directors
    (3) chief accountant
    (4) chief executive officer

71. The degree of importance that an underwriter assigns to certain risk factors varies with the type of insurance that is being underwritten. One risk factor that is usually more important in underwriting individual *life* insurance than in underwriting individual health insurance is the

    (1) proposed insured's occupation
    (2) presence of insurable interest at the time of contract formation
    (3) tendency of people with a greater-than-average likelihood of loss to apply for insurance coverage
    (4) danger that a proposed insured might deliberately attempt to conceal or to misrepresent pertinent information

72. Within an insurance company's information system, data is defined as being *nonredundant* if it

    (1) appears in one file only
    (2) exists unnecessarily in more than one file
    (3) appears a minimum number of times in the data base
    (4) is accessible to one department only

73. Within the brokerage distribution system for insurance products, a *brokerage shop* can be defined as

    (1) a field office operated by a salaried insurance company employee who is charged with encouraging agent-brokers to sell the company's products
    (2) the part of an insurance company's marketing department that is devoted exclusively to developing and maintaining contacts with agent-brokers
    (3) the part of an insurance company's underwriting department that specializes in handling substandard risks
    (4) a field office operated by a general agent who is under contract to a number of insurance companies

74. The McCarran-Ferguson Act declared that life and health insurance companies in the United States are regulated by

    (1) the states, so that Congress retains the right to enact legislation if it feels that state regulation is inadequate
    (2) the states, so that Congress surrenders the right to enact legislation that pertains to the insurance industry
    (3) Congress, so that each state retains the right to enact legislation pertaining to insurance business conducted in that state
    (4) Congress, so that the states surrender the right to enact legislation that pertains to the insurance industry

75. A variety of factors determine whether a manager's span of control in a given situation should be broad or narrow. In general, one true statement about the breadth of a manager's span of control is that the

    (1) simpler and more repetitive subordinates' tasks are, the narrower the manager's span of control should be
    (2) more highly skilled and more competent subordinates are, the narrower the manager's span of control should be
    (3) newer and more untrained subordinates are, the narrower the manager's span of control should be
    (4) greater the manager's own skills and experience, the narrower the manager's span of control should be

END OF EXAMINATION

PRACTICE TEST
COURSE 2
TEXT REFERENCES
AND ANSWER KEY

TEXT: *Operations of Life and Health Insurance Companies*, Second Edition (1992);
Kenneth Huggins, FLMI/M; Robert D. Land, FLMI, ACS

1. c. 4, p. 117	1	38. c. 3, p. 82	1
2. c. 15, p. 419	2	39. c. 11, pp. 311, 313	2
3. c. 6, pp. 177-78	2	40. c. 15, p. 442	1
4. c. 2, p. 36	4	41. c. 11, p. 314	2
5. c. 2, p. 32	3	42. c. 10, p. 298	3
6. c. 17, p. 490	4	43. c. 5, p. 153	2
7. c. 13, pp. 372-73	2	44. c. 8, p. 224	1
8. c. 9, p. 258	3	45. c. 7, pp. 197, 206	2
9. c. 8, p. 217	1	46. c. 3, p. 64	4
10. c. 14, p. 403	4	47. c. 13, p. 375	1
11. c. 14, p. 403	2	48. c. 13, pp. 361, 365-66	3
12. c. 4, p. 122	4	49. c. 9, p. 263	2
13. c. 5, p. 131	1	50. c. 14, p. 398	2
14. c. 1, p. 8	3	51. c. 10, p. 286	1
15. c. 16, p. 462	3	52. c. 15, pp. 417-18	1
16. c. 8, p. 223	4	53. c. 16, p. 457	1
17. c. 2, p. 38	3	54. c. 12, p. 348	3
18. c. 3, p. 76	3	55. c. 9, pp. 246, 251-52	4
19. c. 13, pp. 371-72	1	56. c. 10, p. 272	2
20. c. 16, p. 469	4	57. c. 12, p. 334	4
21. c. 1, p. 28	1	58. c. 1, pp. 14, 18	4
22. c. 15, p. 431	3	59. c. 13, p. 371	4
23. c. 15, p. 438	1	60. c. 9, p. 251	3
24. c. 2, p. 37	3	61. c. 16, p. 454	4
25. c. 17, pp. 484-85	1	62. c. 6, p. 166	4
26. c. 13, p. 363	4	63. c. 7, p. 187	4
27. c. 17, p. 496	3	64. c. 5, p. 135	3
28. c. 9, pp. 249-50	1	65. c. 7, p. 211	3
29. c. 4, p. 110	4	66. c. 4, pp. 104-05	2
30. c. 11, p. 303	1	67. c. 13, p. 367	3
31. c. 15, p. 423	2	68. c. 12, p. 342	2
32. c. 9, pp. 228-29	3	69. c. 12, pp. 327-28, 337	1
33. c. 8, p. 215	2	70. c. 3, p. 67	2
34. c. 9, pp. 240, 242-43	3	71. c. 9, pp. 253, 255	2
35. c. 12, pp. 339, 342	2	72. c. 16, p. 456	3
36. c. 7, p. 203	2	73. c. 6, p. 165	4
37. c. 9, p. 236	4	74. c. 1, p. 13	1
		75. c. 3, p. 71	3

NOTES

NOTES